HOME
SKILLET

# HOME SKILLET

## The Essential Cast Iron Cookbook
## for Easy One-Pan Meals

---

### ROBIN DONOVAN

**ROCKRIDGE PRESS**

For general information on our other products and services or to obtain technical support, please contact our Customer Care Department within the United States at (866) 744-2665, or outside the United States at (510) 253-0500.

Rockridge Press publishes its books in a variety of electronic and print formats. Some content that appears in print may not be available in electronic books, and vice versa.

TRADEMARKS: Rockridge Press and the Rockridge Press logo are trademarks or registered trademarks of Callisto Media Inc. and/or its affiliates, in the United States and other countries, and may not be used without written permission. All other trademarks are the property of their respective owners. Rockridge Press is not associated with any product or vendor mentioned in this book.

COVER PHOTO: Anna_Shepulova/iStock (chicken)

INTERIOR PHOTOS: Stockfood/Clinton Hussey, p.2; Stocksy/David Smart, p.8; Stockfood/The Stepford Husband, p.25; Stocksy/Jeff Wasserman, p.49; Stockfood/People Pictures, p.50; Stockfood/Rua Castilho, p.105; Stocksy/Pixel Stories, p.106; Stocksy/Harald Walker, p.169; Stockfood/Anthony Masterson Photography, p.188.

ISBN: Print 978-1-62315-755-5 | eBook 978-1-62315-756-2

# CONTENTS

# INTRODUCTION

Any avid cook will tell you that there are kitchen tools, and then there are *kitchen tools*, the latter being pieces that are far more than "just cookware." These invaluable items are extensions of the cook's own body, their best friends in the kitchen. For many chefs their knives fall into this category. A good knife is a valuable tool in any cook's arsenal, of course. But even the best of knives can be replaced with a knife of equal—or even better—quality pretty easily.

In my own kitchen, the one irreplaceable tool I cannot do without is my favorite cast iron skillet. That's because it's not just any skillet, but one I've been cooking with for decades. And it's not just that I know it like the back of my hand—which I do—but that every time I use it, something magical happens: It gets better! That's the thing about cast iron cookware: It starts out great but gets better and better the more you use it. How amazing is that?

I'm only slightly embarrassed to admit that I love my cast iron pans so much that I've been known to call them by endearing nicknames. Skillito and Skillie Señor, 10-inch and 14-inch cast iron skillet brothers, have been by my side in the kitchen practically as long as I can remember. I got them soon after leaving my childhood home to go to college, and since then they've moved with me from house to house and city to city; traveled with me on many camping adventures; and cooked more than their share of skillet scones, latkes, mac and cheese, fried chicken, seared steaks, fruit crisps, and gooey chocolate–and–sweetened-condensed-milk concoctions. Like the best of friends, my cast iron skillets are always there for me, willing to take on just about any chore with which I task them.

And cast iron skillets aren't just limited to stove top cooking like frying eggs, griddling pancakes, crisping grilled cheese sandwiches, or simmering stews. They can go straight into a hot oven, as well. I'll sear a steak on the stove top and finish it in the oven, roast a whole chicken, or run the skillet under the broiler to brown the top of a casserole or a sweet streusel topping. I even use my cast iron skillets to bake cakes.

Cast iron cookware has been in use for thousands of years, and with good reason. Besides cast iron's versatility as a cooking surface, it has many other advantages, as well. Cast iron pots and pans are inexpensive and yet, if treated properly, they last forever. And they are true workhorses in the kitchen. For one thing, you could hardly ask for a sturdier cooking vessel. They're made of iron. Enough said, right? No matter how much you abuse a cast iron pan, you'd be hard pressed to cause any real damage. It won't break if you drop it, and its surface doesn't scratch. Leaving it wet might cause it to rust, but that problem is easily remedied. These things were made to last forever, and they do. That's why so many people proudly use cast iron skillets that have been in their families for generations.

But the thing I love most about my cast iron cookware is simple: It works extremely well. Sure, I have fancier cookware, and I won't say it's not lovely, but nothing—really, nothing!—does as much or cooks food as well as a cast iron skillet. Plus you can whip up an entire meal in just one pan, which makes it that much easier to make a delicious home-cooked meal part of my routine any day of the week. My favorite cast iron skillets have earned their place in my kitchen, and that place, more often than not, is on my stove top, ready to be pressed into service at a moment's notice.

Whether you've used your skillet a few times and are looking to shake things up in your kitchen, or you're a seasoned cast iron skillet enthusiast looking for fresh ways to work your skillet, this book is what you need for one-pan meals that are easy yet spectacular. These recipes prove that when all is said and done, your cast iron skillet is the *best* resource for exciting everyday cooking.

# CHAPTER ONE

# YOUR CAST IRON PRIMER

The cast iron skillet holds the peculiar distinction of being one of the most beloved and, at the same time, one of the most anxiety-inducing kitchen tools. Cooks love it because it has an all-natural nonstick coating, is durable, can be heated to very high temperatures, and goes from stove top to oven and back again. But there's no denying that the mention of cast iron cookware incites feelings of fear in some of the most capable cooks. Rest assured, there is no need to fear cast iron. This chapter provides all the information you need to select, care for, and cook with your cast iron skillet today, and for many happy years to come.

## AN AMERICAN TRADITION

If you have any doubt about cast iron's superior abilities in the kitchen, think about the fact that savvy cooks have relied on cookware made of cast iron for more than 2,000 years. The Chinese were using these cooking vessels as far back as the Han Dynasty (206 BC to AD 220).

Though a bit more recent, cast iron cookware's history in the United States is a long and storied one, with cookware being produced in America since the first foundry was established in 1619. Historical documents prove that America's love affair with cast iron cookware has been hot and heavy for centuries.

Take Lewis and Clark and their famous Louisiana Territory expedition early in the nineteenth century. The journal of Joseph Whitehouse, who accompanied Lewis and Clark on the expedition, provides evidence that cast iron Dutch ovens were carried on the journey. Another member of the expedition, John Coulter, held on to his cast iron Dutch oven until his dying days. After his death it sold at auction for $4, the equivalent of a week's pay at the time.

According to historian John G. Ragsdale, George Washington's mother was so fond of her cast iron cookware that she saw fit to bequeath her "cast-iron kitchen furniture," which would have included cookware, in her will dated May 20, 1788.

The cast iron pots used by early Americans were designed to stand on legs over a fire or to hang from hooks above the flames, since most home cooking was done in fireplaces or hearths. When the indoor cooking stove was introduced in the late eighteenth century, cooking pans with flat bottoms, like the skillets, saucepans, and stockpots we use today, became popular.

Until the middle of the twentieth century, virtually all cooking pots and pans were made of cast iron. After World War II, arms factories suddenly found themselves with surpluses of stainless steel and aluminum. At the same time, the baby boom was underway and young homemakers, busy raising families, wanted lightweight, easy-to-care-for cookware. Factories were happy to find a way to make use of their surpluses. By the 1960s, aluminum or steel pans coated with the nonstick coating Teflon became extremely popular and uncoated cookware, including cast iron, fell out of favor. But it didn't disappear. Die-hard fans continued to use their now-vintage cast iron pots and pans, passing them on to the next generation.

Today, cast iron cookware is experiencing a significant resurgence in popularity. Once held in high esteem mostly by grandmothers and antique cookware collectors, the wonders of cast iron are being rediscovered by modern-day foodies, hipster homesteaders, dooms-day preppers, and regular home cooks seeking quality cookware at affordable prices. Some have tired of the constant replacement cycle required by less durable cookware, others are motivated by a desire to lessen their contact with the potentially toxic substances that may be found in synthetic nonstick coatings (see page 12), and others have simply come back around to the age-old understanding that cast iron is one of the best materials for cooking.

## HOW DEEP IS YOUR LOVE?

Ask any dedicated cast iron cookware fan to explain their devotion, and you'll get a litany of answers. It is impossible, really, to say which reason tops the list.

### Superior Heat Conduction

Cast iron gets very, very hot. This is key when cooking certain foods, like meat, which requires very high heat to form a crust that seals in its juices. The very high heat also helps caramelize the sugars in vegetables, fruits, and even meats. Caramelization means deep, rich flavor in your finished dishes. Not only does cast iron get extremely hot, it also retains its heat. While pans made from different materials might drop in temperature the moment you add cold food, cast iron's temperature remains the same.

## Versatility

Cast iron cookware can be used both on the stove top and in a very hot oven, and it can switch gracefully back and forth between the two. You can cook almost anything in it. Yes, it's amazing for searing steaks on the stove top, but you can also pop that baby right into a preheated oven to finish while you put the final touches on your sides. You can use it to cook savory vegetable stir-fries, but you can also use it to bake a cake. How nuts is that?

## Durability

You can drop your cast iron skillet, scrape your metal spatulas against it, leave it out in the sun, or pile a thousand other pans on top of it, but none of these things will leave a dent or a scratch. It's iron, after all. You know, that stuff that's really, really strong. If you leave it lying around wet after washing, it might get a bit rusty, but no worries. Rust is easy to remove, and your pan will soon be good as new.

Cast iron skillets last forever, too. That's exactly why so many people have their grandmother's, or even great-grandmother's cast iron cookware. And they don't keep them just for show, either. These are pans that can be, and are, used on a daily basis for decades.

## Safe, All-Natural Nonstick Surface

These days, many health-conscious cooks are turning to cast iron cookware as a replacement for coated nonstick cooking pans out of concern about the potential for these coatings to leach toxic chemicals into food or to release toxic gases. Nonstick pans are coated with a synthetic polymer called polytetrafluoroetheylene (PTFE), commonly known as Teflon. When heated to high temperatures, this coating can break down and may release toxic fumes. Although manufacturers of nonstick cookware maintain—and many researchers agree—that nonstick coatings are safe as long as you follow the care and usage instructions, switching to cast iron provides peace of mind. No toxic chemicals are used in the production of cast iron cookware, and with good seasoning, you still get a nonstick surface.

### Affordability

As if all of that wasn't enough to make the case for cast iron cookware, this stuff is also surprisingly inexpensive. A good size, quality cast iron skillet will set you back less than $30. Compare that to the cost of more modern cookware, and you'll see what great value cast iron offers.

So what is it that incites such love and devotion for cast iron cookware? Is it the superior heat conduction and distribution, all-natural nonstick surface, versatility, durability, or affordability? The answer for die-hard cast iron cookware fans is all of the above—and more. Simply put, cast iron can tackle just about any cooking task with aplomb, it is safe, it lasts forever, and it is inexpensive. What more could you ask for in a piece of cookware?

## CAST IRON CARE

Properly seasoned and well-cared-for cast iron cookware can last for generations. It can also continue to function as an easy-release surface far longer than modern coated nonstick pans. The key, however, is proper maintenance, and that's where cast iron cookware incites endless debate and anxiety. Everyone knows that cast iron cookware requires maintenance, but what does that mean exactly? So intense is the fear of doing it wrong that some people simply don't use their cast iron cookware at all, letting it idle aimlessly in the cupboard. This section offers all the information you need to properly care for and maintain your cast iron skillet.

### Seasoning a New Skillet

Seasoning is a natural way to give your cast iron cookware a nonstick coating. In simple terms, seasoning means coating the pan with oil and then heating it. This causes the fat to bond to the surface of the pan, giving it a nonstick coating.

The more complicated explanation involves a bit of science. A new cast iron pan will have many tiny cracks, pores, and other surface irregularities. If you cook food in the pan when it is in this state, the food will stick because it will seep into these nooks and crannies.

# 7 Unexpected Ways to Use Your Cast Iron Skillet

The cast iron skillet is the ultimate kitchen workhorse, moving from stove to oven with ease and conducting heat like nobody's business. Griddling pancakes and searing steaks are two obvious uses for your cast iron skillet, but its range doesn't end there. From crispy-skinned roasted chicken to flaky-crusted fruit pies, from meal-in-a-pan casseroles to savory baked breads, the potential of your cast iron skillet is limitless. Use your cast iron skillet in these unexpected ways:

> **QUICK THAWING:** Forgot to thaw your steak for tonight's dinner? No worries. Cast iron will literally pull the cold out of the meat in about an hour. Just put the unwrapped frozen meat directly into the pan and let it sit at room temperature.

> **TENDER MEATS:** One of cast iron's most marked characteristics is its heft. Use this to your advantage and turn your skillet into a meat tenderizer, pounding out chicken, pork, or veal cutlets for dishes like *schnitzel* and *scaloppini*.

> **PERFECT PIZZA:** Because cast iron gets so hot and retains heat so well, it can act like a pizza stone, turning out perfectly crisp, never doughy, pizza crust. Because of its shape, a cast iron skillet is ideal for deep-dish or pan-style pizzas.

> **CRUNCHY GRILLED CHEESE:** Use cast iron's high heat to get that sought-after crunchy exterior for gooey grilled cheese sandwiches. If you are lucky enough to own two cast iron skillets, create a makeshift panini press by placing the second skillet on top of the sandwich as it cooks.

> **ULTIMATE BURGERS:** Heat your cast iron skillet over high heat, sauté onions in it, then push the onions to the side and cook burgers right in the same pan. The result will taste just like those amazing burgers at old-school diners.

> **BAKERY-STYLE BREAD:** Since a cast iron skillet acts like a pizza or baking stone when it's preheated in a very hot oven, your bread will cook quickly and evenly and emerge from the oven with a beautiful golden-brown hue, an airy interior, and a crisp crust.

> **AWARD-WORTHY MAC AND CHEESE:** Baking macaroni and cheese in a cast iron skillet is the most reliable way to get that delectable crunchy edge. You can run it under the broiler, too, to brown a bread crumb topping to a toasty, golden crisp.

Furthermore, due to chemical reactions, proteins in the food will actually bond with the metal causing—you guessed it!—sticking. So the answer is to fill in these little imperfections and create a protective layer between the pan and the food.

When you put a layer of fat over the metal and oxidize it (by heating it in the presence of oxygen), a chemical reaction occurs and the surface of the metal becomes *polymerized*. In other words, the fat bonds with the metal to create a plastic-like coating. This plastic-like coating acts as a nonstick surface. Each time you repeat the process, the coating gets thicker and more effective. Every time you use your pan for oil-based tasks, like searing or frying, another thin layer of this plasticized coating is created, boosting the nonstick qualities of your pan.

If you purchase a new cast iron pan, the box will likely proclaim that it is "pre-seasoned," so you can cook with it right away, but I strongly recommend that you re-season it if you have the time. A good, thick layer of seasoning takes several applications to build.

### SEASONING STEP-BY-STEP:

Follow these steps to season your new cast iron skillet, or re-season one that needs a little love.

1 **Give your pan a good scrub.** Coarse kosher salt makes a great scouring powder that won't damage your pan. Use a hefty amount of kosher salt and a paper towel to scrub off any dust, residue, or rust spots. Wash the pan well with hot water and a mild soap if you wish (I'll address the soap vs. no soap issue in the next section), and then dry it thoroughly.

2 **Preheat the skillet.** Place it in a preheated 200°F oven for 15 minutes. This opens up its pores so it will be more receptive to the oil.

3 **Oil the skillet inside and out.** You can use just about any type of cooking fat to season a skillet, but the best choices are neutral-flavored oils with high smoke points like corn, vegetable, safflower, or flaxseed. Use a paper towel soaked in oil to coat every surface of the skillet.

**4** **Heat the oven to at least 400°F.** (Up to 500°F if your oven goes that high.) Place the skillet on the center rack in the oven upside down (to keep the oil from pooling in the center) and place a baking sheet or piece of aluminum foil below it to catch any dripping oil. Heat the skillet for 1 hour.

**5** **Turn off the oven's heat.** Leave the skillet inside to cool for 2 to 3 hours.

**6** **Repeat steps 2, 3, and 4 several times.** Repeat until your skillet has a deep black, glossy sheen.

**7** **Protect your newly created layer of seasoning.** Avoid cooking acidic foods like tomatoes, wine, vinegar, or lemons/lemon juice in the skillet for the first several times you use it after seasoning. Ideally, the first several dishes you cook in a newly seasoned pan should be those that require you to coat the pan with another layer of fat. Cooking bacon, frying chicken, or making grilled cheese sandwiches are all great ways to bolster your seasoning.

## Cleaning Your Cast Iron

There is a lot of debate about the right way to clean cast iron. The truth is that there are several methods that work well, and different levels of mess can call for different tricks. I've included what I've found to be the five most foolproof methods here. One rule you should always adhere to: Clean your cast iron skillet immediately after use.

**Hot water.** This is by far the simplest and most common cleaning method. If your skillet is well seasoned, food particles should come right off with just a bit of elbow grease, some hot water, and a sponge or a stiff, natural- or plastic-bristle (not wire) brush.

**Boiling water.** If you're having trouble removing stuck-on food, rinse the skillet while it is still hot. Fill the skillet again and bring the water to a boil. Boil for a few minutes to break up stuck-on food. Use a spatula to dislodge food residue, lightly scraping the bottom and sides of the pan. Be careful to do this gently so that you don't scrape off the pan's seasoning layers.

**Kosher salt.** If you are still left with lots of stuck-on food residue, make a paste of coarse kosher salt and warm water and use it as a scrub to scour off stuck-on food.

**Hot, soapy water.** I'm sure you've heard that you should never use soap on your cast iron cookware, but it turns out that this warning is unfounded. Yes, harsh dish soaps are designed to cut through oil, and since seasoning is done with oil, it seems logical that soap would take off your precious seasoning. But in reality, your seasoning is a layer of *polymerized* oil, which, you'll remember, means that the oil has undergone a chemical reaction that has turned it into a plastic-like coating and bonded it to the metal. A dishwashing liquid designed for hand washing won't be able to strip that away. So go ahead and lather up if you like (but do avoid harsh soaps like dishwasher soap.)

## Cast Iron Care—Always and Never

### ALWAYS:

☐ Season a new skillet thoroughly by going through the seasoning process several times before using it to cook.

☐ Clean immediately after use.

☐ Dry immediately after washing.

☐ Rub your skillet with a bit of oil immediately after cleaning and drying it.

☐ Re-season your skillet whenever its surface becomes dull or rusty or food begins to stick to it.

### NEVER:

☐ Put your skillet in the dishwasher.

☐ Use a harsh abrasive like steel wool to scrub your skillet.

☐ Leave your skillet soaking in water for any length of time.

☐ Leave your skillet wet after washing.

☐ Let food sit in your skillet or use it to refrigerate leftover food.

**A raw potato.** Cut a raw potato in half and dip the cut side into either soap or baking soda. Use the cut side of the potato to scrub the skillet well, slicing off the surface and adding more soap or baking soda as needed. This cleaning method is especially effective for ridding your skillet of rust.

When you have finished cleaning and drying your skillet, heat the pan briefly over medium heat and then rub a lightly oil-soaked paper towel over the interior of the skillet. Wipe again with a clean paper towel to remove any excess oil. Allow the pan to cool, and store in a dry place.

## Re-Seasoning Cast Iron

After repeated use, you may notice that food has begun to stick to the surface of your skillet, the finish has become dull, or there is visible rust. These are all signs that it is time to re-season your skillet. To do so, scrub the skillet extremely well with hot, soapy water and a stiff brush or scrubber. In this case, it is okay to use harsher, grease-cutting detergents since your goal is to take the skillet back to its pre-seasoned state. Rinse the skillet and dry it well.

If you notice rust beginning to form, submerge the skillet in a solution made of one part distilled vinegar and one part cold water. After a few minutes, the rust should begin to bubble off. Rinse and dry the skillet thoroughly.

Now that you have brought your skillet back to its original, unseasoned state, immediately revisit the seasoning steps in the previous section, beginning with step 2. As before, repeat steps 2, 3, and 4 several times to recreate a deep black, glossy sheen.

Since your pan now has an entirely new layer of seasoning, you'll again want to avoid cooking acidic foods for the first several uses, leaning instead toward uses that require the skillet to become coated with oil.

# Cast Iron Myths

Myths about cast iron cookware abound. Here are the top five debunked:

### MYTH #1: CAST IRON COOKWARE IS DIFFICULT TO MAINTAIN.

Cast iron care may be different than that of other cookware, but if you treat it right—which is incredibly easy, involving simple steps to season it properly and keep it clean and dry—your cast iron cookware can last for decades (or even longer!). Just follow the seasoning or re-seasoning instructions in this chapter for a lifetime of delicious meals.

### MYTH #2: CAST IRON COOKWARE CAN NEVER BE WASHED WITH SOAP.

The magical nonstick surface of a cast iron skillet is created by a thin coating of oil. Dish soap is designed specifically to cut through oil and grease. It's easy to see why this myth persists. However, the seasoning layer is created by a chemical process that transforms that thin layer of oil into a plastic-like layer that is bonded to the metal. A bit of dish soap won't cut through that.

### MYTH #3: CAST IRON CAN'T BE USED TO COOK ACIDIC FOODS.

In theory, iron may leech into your food when cooking with acidic ingredients, leading to meals with an unpleasant flavor and even potentially harming your health over time. In reality, if your skillet is properly seasoned, food only comes into contact with the seasoning layer, not the metal. However, when your seasoning layer is new, it's a good idea to avoid cooking acidic foods, like tomato-based sauces, just until the seasoning is well established. After that, a bit of acid won't harm your food, or your health.

### MYTH #4: ALL CAST IRON COOKWARE IS THE SAME, WHETHER IT'S OLD OR NEW.

If you've noticed that you can't seem to make your modern cast iron cookware as nonstick as the skillet you inherited from your great-grandmother, you're on to something. Although the process of making cast iron cookware hasn't changed much over the last few hundred years, it has been simplified for economy. Vintage pans have a smooth, satiny finish because their pebbly surfaces were polished smooth at the factory. After World War II, manufacturers streamlined their production process, dropping this step completely. By diligently seasoning your pan, you can achieve a very nice nonstick surface, but you'll have to accept that your modern cast iron skillet will never rival the smoothness of great-grandma's.

### MYTH #5: YOU CAN'T USE METAL UTENSILS IN A CAST IRON SKILLET.

Cast iron seasoning does not act like the Teflon coating of modern nonstick pans. It's nearly impossible to scrape off the seasoning with a spatula, especially through normal cooking. The layer of seasoning on your cast iron cookware is actually much more resilient than Teflon and other synthetic nonstick coatings. Through the seasoning process, the oil becomes bonded to the metal. So go ahead and use those metal utensils!

## PERFECT ONE-PAN MEALS

One of the best tips for keeping your cast iron skillet in the best possible shape is also the simplest: Use it! And I'm not just talking about using it once in a while, either. The more you use your cast iron cookware, the better it will get. And what serendipity that a cast iron skillet just happens to be a piece of cookware that can handle a multitude of different tasks, making it a cooking tool that you'll find useful for every meal of every day.

# A Cast Iron Enthusiast

If, like me, you find yourself using your cast iron skillet all the time, you may want to expand your collection. You could go crazy, but what are the best pieces to round out a small but useful collection? Here's what I recommend:

**10-INCH SKILLET.** The perfect starter piece, this one's a good size for different types of dishes. It's not too heavy, and you can find a good-quality one for under $30.

**12-INCH SKILLET.** This larger skillet comes in handy when cooking for a family. It's not so heavy that it can't be manipulated easily by most cooks, and it will give you a bit more space to load in ingredients.

**LARGE SKILLET.** A 16- or 17-inch size is probably sufficient if you regularly cook dishes that require lots of surface area—say brisket or family-size pizzas. Choose one with two handgrips—given its weight, you'll appreciate the double grip for easier maneuvering and storage.

**DUTCH OVEN.** Great for cooking soups, stews, and chili as well as oven-baked casseroles and braises, these come in multiple sizes, so choose one based on the number of people you regularly cook for.

**REVERSIBLE GRIDDLE/GRILL.** A bit of a specialty piece, the 20-inch-wide reversible griddle/grill that fits over two burners is my second-favorite cast iron tool (after my trusty 10-inch skillet). One side is a ridged grill pan, great for grilling when it's too cold or wet outside; the other side is a flat griddle, handy when making pancakes or home-made tortillas.

Even better, this versatility means that there is no better vessel for cooking one-pan meals. Since you can use it both on the stove top and in the oven, or even on the grill, the possibilities are endless. You can start a dish by sautéing onions and other vegetables on the stove, add grains, meat, and other ingredients, then finish it in the oven.

You can make a pie filling—either a sweet fruit filling or a savory chicken or vegetable pot pie version—on the stove top. Just add a sheet of pastry dough on top and pop it in the oven to bake. You'll be rewarded with a flaky, golden-brown pie that looks as good as it tastes.

Or you can layer sauce, noodles, and cheese, pop it in the oven, and end up with a perfect lasagna, pasta bake, or mac and cheese.

Whether cooking quick stews with chicken, fish, beef, pork, or lamb or hearty bean-and-vegetable or meat-and-grain dishes, the possibilities for one-skillet meals are endless.

## Cast Iron Cooking Tips

Here are my top five tips for cooking in cast iron:

1 **Use plenty of fat**. Seasoning a cast iron pan is important for giving it that nonstick surface we all love. The best way to maintain this seasoning is to use the pan often and use plenty of healthy oil or fat when you cook, as this will bolster your seasoning layer with every use.

2 **Match the burner size to the pan size to ensure even heating**. A too-small or too-large burner won't heat your pan uniformly. If you're using an 8-inch skillet, choose your smallest burner; for a 14-inch or larger skillet, choose the largest.

3 **Always use oven mitts to protect your hands**. Cast iron gets really hot, so don't risk your fingers by using a skimpy dish towel to pull a hot pan from the oven. Invest in a couple of good silicone oven mitts. Some skillets come with silicone handle protectors, or you can buy them separately.

**4 Always use two hands**. Cast iron is heavy, so always use two (protected) hands when lifting a hot cast iron skillet filled with hot food.

**5 Get rid of food smells**. One drawback of cast iron is that it can take on the flavor or smell of the foods cooked in it. If you use your skillet to make a garlicky stir-fry, give it a cursory wipe, and then use it to make a berry crisp, you may end up with a dessert with hints of garlic. If you've cleaned your skillet and it still smells like last night's dinner, place it in a 400°F oven for about 15 minutes. This will cause the smelly compounds to evaporate.

## ABOUT THE RECIPES

I've carefully selected dishes for this book that are especially well suited to cast iron cooking. The curated recipes include some of my favorite skillet dishes, many updated classics, dishes from global cuisines reinvented for the cast iron skillet, and some that use the skillet in new and surprising ways.

To showcase the best features of the cast iron skillet, the recipes here are mainly for one-pan meals. The entire meal is cooked in a single cast iron skillet, which means they're quick and easy to get on the table, and perhaps even better, you'll only have one pan to clean up.

You'll find easy one-skillet dishes suitable for quick and easy breakfasts, lunches, and dinners for busy weekdays, all of which have start-to-finish times of 60 minutes or less. When you're really pressed for time, look for the Quick and Easy label, indicating meals that can be on the table in 30 minutes. The Weekend Meals chapter includes recipes for when you have a little more time to spend in the kitchen. These recipes are still easy and generally require just the one skillet, but they may have longer cooking times or require time for hands-free steps like waiting for meat to marinate or dough to rise.

Most of the recipes are meant to be cooked in a medium-size skillet, either a 10-inch or 12-inch skillet. A few call for a slightly smaller or slightly larger skillet, but they are forgiving enough that even if you only have one or two sizes, you will be able to manage them.

In addition to full-meal-in-a-skillet recipes, you'll find easy recipes for scrumptious sweet and savory breads and rolls, as well as desserts from light fruit crisps to decadent chocolate brownies.

## CHAPTER TWO
# BREAKFAST & BRUNCH

# MAPLE-PECAN AND APPLE OATMEAL BREAKFAST BAKE

SERVES 4 ▪ PREP TIME: 10 MINUTES ▪ COOK TIME: 50 MINUTES

1 cup steel-cut oats

1½ teaspoons ground cinnamon

½ cup chopped pecans

½ teaspoon kosher salt

2 or 3 apples, cut into ½-inch-thick wedges

3½ cups boiling water

3 tablespoons maple syrup, plus more for drizzling

**SEASONAL SWAP:**
*In the fall or winter months, both apples and pears work well in this dish. In the summertime, substitute peaches or nectarines, and in the spring, use strawberries.*

*This hearty breakfast is a great example of the versatility of the cast iron skillet. First you toast the oats and spices in the skillet on the stove top. Next, add fruit and let it begin to caramelize in the hot skillet. Finally, the water is mixed in and the whole thing goes in the oven to cook through and get nicely browned. On a cold winter morning, this breakfast bake is just the thing.*

1 Preheat the oven to 375°F.

2 Heat a 12-inch cast iron skillet over medium heat. Add the oats and cook, stirring constantly, until they give off a toasty aroma, about 3 minutes. Stir in the cinnamon and cook for 1 to 2 minutes more. Stir in the pecans and salt. Add the apples, boiling water, and maple syrup. Stir to mix well, and bring to a boil.

3 Transfer the skillet to the oven and bake for 40 minutes.

4 Serve warm, drizzled with more maple syrup.

# TRIPLE-BERRY BREAKFAST CLAFOUTIS WITH SLICED ALMONDS

SERVES 6 ▪ PREP TIME: 10 MINUTES ▪ COOK TIME: 50 MINUTES

2 tablespoons unsalted butter, melted, plus more at room temperature for greasing

¾ cup sugar

6 tablespoons all-purpose flour

3 eggs, at room temperature

1¼ cups whole milk

2 teaspoons vanilla extract

¼ teaspoon kosher salt

1 cup fresh blueberries

1 cup fresh raspberries

1 cup fresh, quartered strawberries

½ cup sliced almonds

**SEASONAL SWAP:**

*Clafoutis is a versatile dish that can be varied to suit your taste and the season. Peaches, nectarines, apricots, or plums are other good summer fruits to try. In the fall, use pears. In the spring, try strawberries and rhubarb.*

*Clafoutis is usually served as a dessert, but because it lies somewhere between a pancake and an eggy custard and is topped with fresh fruit and almonds, it seems like fair game for breakfast or brunch to me. Serve it with a dollop of yogurt, and you can feel perfectly virtuous.*

1  Preheat the oven to 350°F.

2  Generously grease a 12-inch cast iron skillet with the room-temperature butter.

3  In a blender or food processor, process the melted butter, sugar, flour, eggs, milk, vanilla, and salt until smooth.

4  Pour the batter into the prepared skillet, and scatter the blueberries, raspberries, and strawberries over the batter, distributing them evenly. Scatter the almonds over the top in an even layer.

5  Bake until the custard is set and a tester inserted in the center comes out clean, 35 to 45 minutes.

6  Let cool for a few minutes, slice into wedges, and serve warm.

# LEMON DUTCH BABY WITH BLUEBERRY SAUCE

SERVES 6 ▪ PREP TIME: 5 MINUTES ▪ COOK TIME: 30 MINUTES

## FOR THE DUTCH BABY

3 eggs, at room temperature

⅔ cup whole milk, at room temperature

⅔ cup all-purpose flour

2 teaspoons finely grated lemon zest

½ teaspoon vanilla extract

⅛ teaspoon ground cinnamon

⅛ teaspoon kosher salt

4 tablespoons unsalted butter, cut into pieces

## FOR THE BLUEBERRY SAUCE

⅓ cup sugar

1 tablespoon cornstarch

¼ teaspoon ground cinnamon

¼ cup water

1½ cups fresh blueberries

*A Dutch baby (also called a German pancake) is similar to a clafoutis but is puffier, more akin to a popover than a custard. Unlike clafoutis, Dutch babies are almost exclusively served for breakfast and are more likely to be simply flavored with cinnamon and other spices and served plain or dusted with powdered sugar. This version includes a simple blueberry sauce poured over the top, adding a spot of intense color and flavor to your morning meal.*

**To make the Dutch baby**

1 Place a 10-inch cast iron skillet in the oven and preheat the oven to 450°F.

2 In a medium bowl using an electric mixer or in a stand mixer, beat the eggs at high speed until they become frothy and pale yellow. Add the milk, flour, lemon zest, vanilla, cinnamon, and salt, and beat until smooth.

3 Remove the preheated skillet from the oven and add the butter to it, swirling to coat the bottom of the pan. Pour the batter into the skillet and return it to the preheated oven.

4 Bake for 18 to 25 minutes, until it puffs up and turns golden brown.

**To make the blueberry sauce and serve**

1  While the pancake is in the oven, in a large glass measuring cup or microwave-safe bowl, stir well to combine the sugar, cornstarch, cinnamon, water, and blueberries. Microwave on high, stirring every couple of minutes, until the mixture begins to boil and thickens, about 4 minutes total.

2  Cut the Dutch baby into wedges, and serve warm with the sauce drizzled over the top.

SEASONAL SWAP:
*You can use either fresh or frozen blueberries for the sauce, but if they're not in season and you don't have any in your freezer, simply top the Dutch baby with a mixture of ⅓ cup sugar and 2 teaspoons finely grated lemon zest.*

# CARAMELIZED BANANA AND COCONUT QUINOA SKILLET

SERVES 6 ▪ PREP TIME: 10 MINUTES ▪ COOK TIME: 40 MINUTES

¼ cup coconut oil, divided

3 medium bananas, sliced

1 cup quinoa

2 cups very hot water

¼ teaspoon kosher salt

½ cup chopped dates

¼ cup shredded, unsweetened coconut

3 tablespoons brown sugar, divided

2 teaspoons ground cinnamon, divided

1 cup chopped toasted pecans

*Quinoa is truly a wonder grain. It eats like a carb but is loaded with protein and minerals. Sweetened with dates, bananas, and brown sugar, this hearty breakfast is a delicious way to start the day and has enough nutrition to keep you going until lunchtime. The leftovers are tasty served at room temperature or warmed up. I like to make a big batch on Sunday and eat it for breakfast all week.*

1  Preheat the oven to 375°F.

2  In a 10-inch cast iron skillet over medium heat, heat 2 tablespoons of coconut oil. Add the banana slices in a single layer and cook until browned on the bottom, about 2 minutes. Flip the banana slices over and cook until browned on the second side, 1 to 2 minutes more. Remove the bananas from the skillet and set aside.

3  In the skillet over medium heat, heat the remaining 2 tablespoons of coconut oil. Add the quinoa and stir well to ensure all the grains are coated with oil. Cook, stirring occasionally, for 3 minutes, then add the hot water and salt. Increase the heat to high and bring the liquid to a boil. Reduce the heat so that the liquid is at a low simmer, and cook for about 10 minutes.

4  Stir in the dates, coconut, half of the browned banana slices, 1 tablespoon of brown sugar, and 1 teaspoon of cinnamon. Remove the skillet from the heat and spread the mixture out into an even layer.

5  In a small bowl, stir together the pecans, the remaining 2 tablespoons of brown sugar, and the remaining 1 teaspoon of cinnamon. Sprinkle the nut mixture evenly over the quinoa mixture, and top with the remaining browned bananas.

6  Transfer the skillet to the oven and bake until the top turns golden brown, about 20 minutes.

7  Serve hot.

**SEASONAL SWAP:** *In the summertime, you could substitute peaches or nectarines for the bananas. In the fall, apples or pears would work nicely.*

# VANILLA-ORANGE ALMOND SKILLET CAKE

SERVES 8 ▪ PREP TIME: 10 MINUTES ▪ COOK TIME: 25 MINUTES

6 tablespoons unsalted butter, melted and cooled, plus more at room temperature, for greasing

1 cup sugar

4 oranges, divided (1 zested and juiced, 3 zested, peeled, and sliced into ⅛-inch-thick rounds)

2 eggs

1 teaspoon vanilla extract

½ teaspoon almond extract

¼ teaspoon kosher salt

¾ cup all-purpose flour

¼ cup almond meal

½ teaspoon baking powder

¼ cup sliced almonds

**SEASONAL SWAP:**

*In the springtime, substitute 2 cups of sliced fresh strawberries for the orange slices.*

*Cake for breakfast? This one is loaded with heart-healthy almonds and oranges, so I'm pretty sure Mom would approve. This moist cake is easy to whip up using just one bowl and your trusty 10-inch cast iron skillet. Try serving it topped with a dollop of vanilla yogurt and fresh fruit.*

1 Preheat the oven to 350°F.

2 Generously grease a 10-inch cast iron skillet with the room-temperature butter.

3 In a medium bowl, mix the sugar and orange zest together using your hands until the sugar is moist. Add the eggs, one at a time, whisking to incorporate after each addition. Add the vanilla, almond extract, salt, and orange juice.

4 Add the flour, almond meal, and baking powder to the bowl. Use a rubber spatula to fold the ingredients together until well combined. Add the melted butter and continue folding until well incorporated.

5 Transfer the batter to the prepared skillet, and sprinkle the sliced almonds evenly over the batter. Arrange the orange slices on top of the batter in a single layer.

6 Transfer the skillet to the oven and bake until golden brown, 22 to 25 minutes. Let cool in the skillet for 5 minutes before running a knife around the sides of the cake to separate it from the sides of the skillet.

7 Cool completely, cut into wedges, and serve at room temperature.

# ONE BIG CINNAMON ROLL

SERVES 6 TO 8 ▪ PREP TIME: 45 MINUTES, PLUS ABOUT 2 HOURS TO RISE
COOK TIME: 30 MINUTES

## FOR THE DOUGH

1 cup whole milk

½ cup plus 1 teaspoon sugar, divided

1½ teaspoons kosher salt

1 cup warm water

2 packets (4½ teaspoons) active dry yeast

2 eggs, at room temperature

5 to 6 cups all-purpose flour, divided

4 tablespoons unsalted butter, melted, plus more at room temperature, for greasing

## FOR THE FILLING

1 cup sugar

½ cup dark brown sugar

1 tablespoon ground cinnamon

½ cup (1 stick) unsalted butter, melted

## FOR THE GLAZE

2 cups powdered sugar

2 tablespoons milk

1 teaspoon vanilla extract

*I couldn't imagine a cast iron skillet cookbook without this delectable breakfast pastry. It looks stunning out of the oven, and once you bite into the sweet and spicy glazed pastry, you'll agree it is worth the effort. To save time, make the dough, form the roll, and let it rise up to a day ahead, and refrigerate, covered, until ready to bake. Remove it from the refrigerator about 45 minutes before baking to allow it to come to room temperature.*

**To make the dough**

1  In a microwave-safe bowl or measuring cup, combine the milk, ½ cup of sugar, and the salt and heat in the microwave for 30 seconds at a time, stirring in between, until the sugar is dissolved and the milk is hot.

2  In a large mixing bowl or the bowl of a stand mixer, stir together the warm water, yeast, and the remaining 1 teaspoon of sugar. Set aside until the mixture becomes foamy, about 10 minutes.

3  Add the eggs to the yeast mixture, and beat with a handheld electric mixer, the paddle attachment of your stand mixer, or a wooden spoon. Add 2 cups of flour and mix (with the dough hook, if you have one) until incorporated. Add an additional 2 cups of flour and mix until the dough is smooth and elastic. Add the melted butter and mix until incorporated. Add the remaining 1 to 2 cups of flour, as needed, ¼ cup at a time, until the dough begins to pull away from the sides of the bowl. The dough should be soft, supple, and still a bit sticky. Knead the dough (either with the dough hook or by hand on a lightly floured board) for 5 minutes. ➧➧

4 Grease a large bowl with the room-temperature butter and add the dough to it, turning the dough to coat with the butter. Cover the bowl and set it in a warm spot on your countertop to rise until doubled in size, about 1 hour.

**To make the filling and bake the roll**

1 Meanwhile, in a small bowl, stir to combine the sugar, brown sugar, and cinnamon.

2 When the dough has doubled in size, punch it down and transfer it to a lightly floured surface, kneading it a few times. Divide the dough into two equal-size pieces, and roll each piece out into a 9-by-12-inch rectangle.

3 Brush each rectangle generously with the melted butter, and sprinkle the cinnamon-sugar mixture evenly over each rectangle.

4 Cut each rectangle into 5 long strips of equal width. Roll the first strip into a tight spiral, and place it in the center of a lightly buttered 12-inch cast iron skillet. Use the next strip to continue the spiral. Continue wrapping the dough strips around in a spiral pattern until you have used them all up. Cover with a clean dish towel and let rise in a warm spot on your countertop until doubled in size, about 45 minutes.

5 During this second rise, preheat the oven to 400°F. Bake the cinnamon roll until the top turns deep golden brown, 25 to 30 minutes.

**To make the glaze and serve**

1 In a medium bowl, whisk together the powdered sugar, milk, and vanilla until smooth. Pour the glaze over the hot cinnamon roll in the skillet.

2 Cut into wedges and serve warm.

# CANDIED GINGER AND PEACH SCONES

SERVES 8 ■ PREP TIME: 15 MINUTES ■ COOK TIME: 15 MINUTES

2 ¼ cups unbleached pastry flour or unbleached all-purpose flour

⅓ cup sugar

1 tablespoon baking powder

¾ cup (1 ½ sticks) unsalted butter, cut into small pieces and chilled

Finely grated zest of about ½ lemon (about 1 teaspoon)

⅔ cup finely chopped candied ginger

¾ cup heavy cream, plus more for brushing

2 tablespoons raw or Turbinado sugar

**SEASONAL SWAP:**

*If peaches aren't in season, you could use frozen peaches. Pears or apples would also be a delicious substitute.*

QUICK & EASY

*Candied ginger lends intriguing flavor to these quick and easy scones. Juicy peaches keep them moist, and their sweetness balances the ginger's kick. Golden brown on the top with a crisp shell on the bottom, thanks to the great heat conduction abilities of cast iron, these will disappear quickly. (Hint: you might want to make 2 batches!)*

1 Preheat the oven to 400°F.

2 In a large bowl using a handheld electric mixer, in a stand mixer fitted with the paddle attachment, or in a food processor fitted with the steel blade, process the flour, sugar, and baking powder to mix. Add the butter and lemon zest, and pulse until the mixture resembles a fine meal.

3 In a large bowl, stir the ginger into the flour mixture. Form a well in the center of the mixture and pour the cream into the hole. Using your hands, mix the dry ingredients into the cream just until combined.

4 With clean hands, knead the dough a few times on a lightly floured surface, then form it into a ball. Transfer the dough into a 10-inch cast iron skillet, and pat it out until it covers the bottom of the skillet and is about ¾-inch thick. Brush the top with a bit of the remaining cream, sprinkle the raw sugar over the top, and bake until the top begins to brown, about 15 minutes.

5 Let cool in the pan for a few minutes before slicing into wedges. Serve warm or at room temperature.

# UPSIDE-DOWN CARAMEL-APPLE COFFEE CAKE

SERVES 8 ▪ PREP TIME: 10 MINUTES ▪ COOK TIME: 30 MINUTES

## FOR THE CARAMEL APPLES

½ cup (1 stick) unsalted butter, at room temperature

¾ cup sugar

4 large Granny Smith apples, peeled, cored, and sliced into wedges

## FOR THE CAKE

½ cup (1 stick) unsalted butter at room temperature

1 cup sugar

2 large eggs

2 cups all-purpose flour

2 teaspoons baking powder

¾ teaspoon ground cinnamon

½ teaspoon fine sea salt

⅔ cup sour cream

2 teaspoons vanilla extract

1 Granny Smith apple, peeled, cored, and diced small

*Uh oh. Here we go again: cake for breakfast. But this one is chock-full of fresh apples and is the perfect accompaniment to that first hot cup of java on a crisp fall morning. See what I did there? It's not cake; it's coffee cake. That automatically qualifies it as a breakfast food, right?*

Preheat the oven to 375°F.

**To make the caramel apples**

1 In a 10-inch cast iron skillet over low heat, melt the butter. Add the sugar, stirring to incorporate it into the melted butter.

2 Arrange the apple slices on their cut sides in the skillet, and continue to cook over low heat while you prepare the cake batter.

**To make the cake and serve**

1 In a large bowl, beat the butter with an electric mixer at medium speed until it is creamy, 2 to 3 minutes. With the mixer still running, add the sugar and beat for another 2 to 3 minutes. Add the eggs, one at a time, beating after each addition until incorporated.

2 In a medium bowl, mix together the flour, baking powder, cinnamon, and salt.

3 Add the flour mixture to the butter mixture in several additions, beating with the electric mixer after each addition to incorporate. Add the sour cream and vanilla, and beat on low until incorporated. Stir in the diced apple with a spoon.

4 Remove the skillet from the heat, and pour the batter over the apples. Using the back of a spoon or an offset spatula, spread the batter out to an even layer. Bake until the cake is golden brown on top, 20 to 25 minutes.

5 Remove the skillet from the oven and let the cake cool in the pan for several minutes, then run a knife around the side of the cake to release it. Carefully invert the cake onto a serving platter, cut into wedges, and serve warm or at room temperature.

# CHARD, SCALLION, AND GOAT CHEESE FRITTATA

SERVES 6 ▪ PREP TIME: 5 MINUTES ▪ COOK TIME: 15 MINUTES

2 tablespoons extra-virgin olive oil, divided

6 scallions, chopped

8 large leaves Swiss chard, leaves julienned, stems finely diced, leaves and stems divided

½ teaspoon kosher salt

3 garlic cloves, minced

8 eggs

4 ounces crumbled goat cheese

**PERFECT PAIRING:**

*For a lovely brunch dish, serve this frittata with a salad of baby greens tossed in a tangy citrus vinaigrette and/or some nice crusty bread.*

*The beauty of frittata is that it is delicious served hot, warm, or at room temperature, making it a great dish for everything from a festive brunch to a busy weekday morning breakfast. This simple version has only a handful of ingredients, but you can add other vegetables you have on hand or switch up the cheese if you like. You might even add diced Spanish chorizo or bacon.*

1 In a 10-inch cast iron skillet over medium heat, heat 1 tablespoon of olive oil. Add the scallions and cook, stirring frequently, until they soften, about 3 minutes. Add the chard leaves and salt and cook, stirring frequently, for about 2 minutes more, until the greens wilt. Stir in the chard stems and the garlic. Remove from the heat.

2 In a large bowl, whisk the eggs. Add the vegetable mixture and the cheese, and stir to mix.

3 Preheat the broiler.

4 Wipe out the skillet and add the remaining 1 tablespoon of olive oil. Heat over medium-high heat. Pour in the egg mixture and cook just until the eggs set on the bottom, about 4 minutes.

5 Transfer the skillet to the broiler and cook until the eggs are set in the center and the top is golden brown, about 3 minutes.

6 Run a knife around the sides of the frittata to release it from the skillet, then carefully (using oven mitts on both hands) invert it onto a serving platter. Cut into wedges and serve hot, warm, or at room temperature.

# RICOTTA FRITTATA WITH SORREL

SERVES 6 ▪ PREP TIME: 5 MINUTES ▪ COOK TIME: 15 MINUTES

2 tablespoons extra-virgin
olive oil, divided

½ onion, diced

3 garlic cloves, minced

8 large leaves sorrel, chopped

½ teaspoon kosher salt

8 eggs

¾ cup ricotta cheese

Freshly ground black pepper

**SEASONAL SWAP:**
*If you can't find sorrel
in your market, sub-
stitute baby spinach
and whisk the zest of
1 lemon into the eggs.*

*Sorrel is a leafy green herb that appears in farmers'
markets and some better supermarkets in the spring
and summer. It is similar in texture to spinach but has a
distinctive tangy flavor that some people liken to the flavor
of lemons. Here it brings a bright note to a simple frittata
made with onions, garlic, and creamy ricotta cheese.*

1 In a 10-inch cast iron skillet, heat 1 tablespoon of olive
oil. Add the onion and garlic and cook, stirring frequently,
until softened, about 5 minutes. Add the sorrel and salt
and cook, stirring frequently, for 1 to 2 minutes more,
until the greens wilt. Remove from the heat.

2 In a large bowl, whisk the eggs. Add the onion and
sorrel mixture, and stir to mix.

3 Preheat the broiler.

4 Wipe out the skillet. Over medium-high heat, heat the
remaining 1 tablespoon of oil. Pour in the egg mixture.
Dollop the ricotta on top by the heaping spoonful, distributing it evenly on top of the eggs, and cook just until the
eggs set on the bottom, about 4 minutes.

5 Transfer the skillet to the broiler and cook until the
eggs are set in the center and the top is golden brown,
about 3 minutes.

6 Run a knife around the sides of the frittata to release
it from the skillet, then carefully (using oven mitts on
both hands) invert it onto a serving platter. Sprinkle with
freshly ground pepper, cut into wedges, and serve hot,
warm, or at room temperature.

# SPICY HUEVOS RANCHEROS

SERVES 4 ▪ PREP TIME: 10 MINUTES ▪ COOK TIME: 20 MINUTES

3 tablespoons extra-virgin olive oil, divided

½ onion, diced

2 garlic cloves, minced

2 large tomatoes, diced, divided

2 cups cooked pinto beans or 1 (15-ounce) can, rinsed and drained

2 tablespoons water

1 teaspoon ground coriander

1 teaspoon ground cumin

½ teaspoon ground chipotle powder

½ teaspoon ground smoked paprika

½ teaspoon kosher salt

Freshly ground black pepper

4 (6-inch) corn tortillas

4 eggs

½ cup crumbled Cotija, queso fresco, feta, or goat cheese

1 large avocado, sliced

2 tablespoons chopped fresh cilantro

Hot sauce, for garnish

1 lime, cut into wedges

Huevos rancheros—*rancher's eggs*—*is the kind of traditional, hearty morning meal you'd expect to find on a farm in rural Mexico. Toasted tortillas are topped with seasoned beans, fried eggs, cheese, and usually some sort of hot sauce and garnishes like avocado or guacamole. This version is made all in one skillet, and the eggs are baked on top of the beans, so the whole dish melds together perfectly.*

1 Preheat the oven to 400°F.

2 In a 12-inch cast iron skillet over medium-high heat, heat 2 tablespoons of olive oil. Add the onion and cook, stirring frequently, until softened, about 5 minutes. Stir in the garlic and continue to cook, stirring, for 1 more minute.

3 Add three-quarters of the tomatoes, the beans, water, coriander, cumin, chipotle powder, paprika, and salt, and season with pepper. Reduce the heat to medium-low and bring to a simmer. Cook, stirring occasionally, for 5 minutes more. Transfer the bean mixture to a large bowl, and wipe out the skillet.

4  Add the remaining 1 tablespoon of olive oil to the skillet and swirl to coat the bottom and sides. Arrange the tortillas in the skillet in a single layer (they may overlap a little). Spread the bean mixture evenly over the tortillas. Using the back of a spoon, make four wells in the beans. Crack an egg into each well. Sprinkle salt and pepper over each egg, and crumble the cheese over the top.

5  Transfer the skillet to the oven and bake until the eggs are cooked to your liking and the whole thing is bubbling and hot, about 10 minutes.

6  Serve immediately, giving each person a tortilla and an egg along with beans and sauce. Garnish with the avocado slices, cilantro, hot sauce, the remaining chopped tomato, and the lime wedges.

# SOUTHWESTERN SAVORY CORN CAKES

SERVES 4 ▪ PREP TIME: 10 MINUTES ▪ COOK TIME: 25 MINUTES

1 cup finely ground corn meal

½ cup all-purpose flour

1 teaspoon kosher salt

1 teaspoon ground cumin

2 eggs

1½ cups plain, whole-milk yogurt

Kernels from 2 ears of corn or about 2 cups frozen (thawed) corn

2 red or green jalapeño or serrano peppers, seeded and diced

¼ cup minced fresh cilantro

4 ounces shredded sharp white Cheddar cheese

2 tablespoons vegetable oil

Salsa or hot sauce, for serving (optional)

**PERFECT PAIRING:**

*Serve these savory cakes with classic Mexican garnishes like sliced avocado, guacamole, additional shredded cheese, and pickled chiles.*

*These cakes make a great quick and savory breakfast when you want to get going in a hurry. You can use any type of cheese you like. A sharp white Cheddar is a great choice, but a tangy goat cheese or a creamy Monterey Jack would be equally delicious. For a heartier meal, you can serve these cakes topped with fried eggs along with sausage or bacon.*

1 In a medium bowl, whisk together the corn meal, flour, salt, and cumin. Add the eggs and whisk to combine well. Stir in the yogurt, corn, peppers, cilantro, and cheese.

2 In a 12-inch cast iron skillet over medium-high heat, heat the vegetable oil. Ladle about ¼ cup of batter into the pan, flattening the mound with the back of the ladle or spoon to make a circle about 4 inches across and ¼-inch thick. You should be able to fit about 4 of these in the skillet at a time. Cook until the cakes are golden brown on the bottom, about 3 minutes. Flip the cakes over and cook until crisp and browned, 2 to 3 minutes more. Drain on paper towels. Repeat with the remaining batter.

3 Serve hot, topped with salsa (if using).

# CRISPY POTATO PANCAKE WITH SMOKED SALMON AND CHIVES

SERVES 4 ▪ PREP TIME: 10 MINUTES ▪ COOK TIME: 25 MINUTES

1½ pounds potatoes (Yukon Golds or russets), peeled and grated using the large holes of a box grater or a food processor

2 teaspoons kosher salt

Freshly ground black pepper

¼ cup vegetable oil

12 ounces sliced lox (smoked salmon)

½ cup crème fraîche or sour cream

2 tablespoons snipped chives

**PERFECT PAIRING:**

*Go one step further and top each serving with chopped cucumber and fresh dill. For an extra-special brunch, serve glasses of crisp bubbly or mimosas with this dish.*

*This big potato pancake looks impressive coming out of the pan. Cut into wedges and top each serving with crème fraîche or sour cream and slivers of melt-in-your-mouth smoked salmon for an elegant brunch dish.*

1  In a large bowl, toss the potatoes with the salt and season with pepper. Let rest for 5 minutes.

2  With your hands, squeeze out as much water as you can, transferring the potatoes to a separate large, dry bowl as you go.

3  In a 10-inch cast iron skillet over medium-high heat, heat the vegetable oil. When the oil is very hot, add the shredded potatoes by the handful, breaking up any clumps as you go. Continue until all of the potatoes are in the skillet, and use a fork to spread them into an even layer. Cook until the bottom turns a deep golden and the potatoes on top begin to soften and become translucent, about 15 minutes.

4  To turn the pancake over, slide it onto a large dinner plate and then carefully invert the plate over the skillet. Cook until the second side is deep golden brown and the potatoes are tender throughout, about 8 more minutes.

5  Cut the potato cake into wedges, and serve topped with slices of lox, dollops of crème, and a sprinkling of chives.

# SWEET POTATO HASH WITH CARAMELIZED ONIONS AND SAUSAGE

SERVES 4 ▪ PREP TIME: 10 MINUTES ▪ COOK TIME: 35 MINUTES

2 tablespoons extra-virgin olive oil

2 tablespoons butter

1 large onion, thinly sliced

2 garlic cloves, minced

2 large sweet potatoes, peeled and diced

1 teaspoon kosher salt, plus more for sprinkling

¼ teaspoon freshly ground black pepper, plus more for sprinkling

¼ teaspoon ground paprika

5 cooked breakfast sausage links (use any type of sausage you like, from maple chicken to a traditional pork breakfast sausage, Italian sausage, or even chorizo)

1 cup kale, ribs removed, leaves julienned

2 tablespoons chopped fresh flat-leaf parsley

4 eggs

¼ cup shredded cheese, divided

*This savory meal-in-a-skillet is a satisfying breakfast or brunch. It also makes a mighty fine "breakfast for dinner" meal. If you like your hash and eggs spicy, go ahead and drizzle a bit of hot sauce over the top. Use your favorite shredded cheese for a personal touch, or whatever kind you have handy for simplicity.*

1 Preheat the oven to 400°F.

2 In a 12-inch cast iron skillet over medium-high heat, heat the olive oil and butter. Add the onion and cook, stirring frequently and reducing the heat to medium if needed to keep it from burning, until soft and golden brown, about 10 minutes.

3 Add the garlic, sweet potatoes, salt, pepper, and paprika, and stir to mix well. Cook, stirring frequently, until the sweet potatoes are soft and beginning to brown, 10 to 15 minutes more.

4 Add the sausage, kale, and parsley, and cook until the kale is tender and the sausage is hot, about 5 minutes more.

5 Make 4 indentations in the hash, and crack an egg into each. Sprinkle salt, pepper, and 1 tablespoon of shredded cheese over each egg.

6 Transfer the skillet to the oven, and cook until the eggs are cooked to your liking, 3 to 5 minutes.

7 Serve each person one egg along with the surrounding "nest" of hash.

**DID YOU KNOW?**
*There is a lot of confusion about what constitutes a yam versus a sweet potato, since the names are often used interchangeably here in the United States. In truth, real yams, which are native to Africa and Asia, are nearly impossible to find in this country. For this recipe, choose the type of sweet potato that has reddish-brown skin and bright orange flesh—which may very well be labeled a yam in your market.*

# BAKED EGGS WITH SPINACH, MUSHROOMS, AND BACON

SERVES 4 ▪ PREP TIME: 10 MINUTES ▪ COOK TIME: 20 MINUTES

2 (10-ounce) packages fresh spinach, chopped

4 strips bacon, diced

1 onion, finely chopped

6 ounces mushrooms (cremini, chanterelle, morel, shiitake, button, or an assortment), thinly sliced

1 garlic clove, minced

⅓ cup heavy cream

⅛ teaspoon freshly grated nutmeg

Kosher salt

Freshly ground black pepper

4 eggs

2 tablespoons finely grated Parmesan cheese (½ ounce)

*Serving eggs to a crowd can be a challenge. This complete one-skillet breakfast solves the problem gracefully. A savory bacon and vegetable mix is sautéed in the skillet and topped with eggs, then the whole thing goes into the oven to bake. Pop some bread in the toaster, and by the time it's golden brown, you've got a nutritious, full breakfast for everyone at the table. This recipe is easily doubled using a large skillet.*

1 Preheat the oven to 450°F.

2 Heat a 10-inch cast iron skillet over medium heat. Add the spinach and cook about 2 minutes, stirring occasionally, until wilted. Press down on the spinach to release as much water as possible. Remove to a paper towel–lined plate to drain.

3 Drain the water from the skillet and wipe it dry. Return it to medium heat.

4 Add the bacon and cook, stirring, until it begins to brown, about 3 minutes. Add the onion and cook, stirring frequently, until soft, about 3 minutes.

5 Increase the heat to medium-high, add the mushrooms and cook, stirring, until they release their liquid and become soft, about 4 minutes. Stir in the garlic and cook until fragrant, about 1 minute more. Stir in the cream, nutmeg, and spinach. Season with salt and pepper, and cook until the mixture comes to a simmer. Remove the skillet from the heat.

6 With the back of a spoon, create 4 wells in the spinach and break an egg into each. Sprinkle salt, pepper, and cheese over the eggs, and transfer the skillet to the oven. Bake until the egg whites are set but the yolks are still a bit runny, about 8 minutes.

7 Serve immediately.

# CHAPTER THREE

# WEEKNIGHT MEALS

Getting dinner on the table on top of everything else you have to juggle any given weekday can be a challenge, which is why I like to identify those perfectly quick and simple meals that keep everyone fed and satisfied with minimal effort. The recipes in this chapter all have start-to-finish times of 60 minutes or less. Look for the Quick & Easy label for recipes that are ready in under 30 minutes.

# VEGETARIAN

## WEEKNIGHT MEALS

# VEGETARIAN BIRYANI WITH CHARRED ONIONS AND RAITA

SERVES 4 ▪ PREP TIME: 10 MINUTES ▪ COOK TIME: 35 MINUTES

## FOR THE BIRYANI

2 tablespoons vegetable oil, plus more if needed

1 large onion, half diced, half thinly sliced, divided

1 teaspoon kosher salt, plus a pinch

2 garlic cloves, minced

1 jalapeño pepper, chopped

1 tablespoon minced fresh ginger (about a 1-inch piece)

1½ teaspoons garam masala

½ teaspoon ground coriander

¼ teaspoon ground turmeric

1 medium tomato, chopped, or ½ cup canned diced tomatoes

2 carrots, diced

1 cup green beans, cut into 1½-inch pieces

1 cup shelled green peas

1 cup basmati rice, rinsed and drained

2½ cups water

## FOR THE RAITA

½ cup plain, whole-milk yogurt

1 cucumber, peeled, seeded, and grated

½ teaspoon kosher salt

¼ teaspoon ground cumin

*This Indian rice dish is traditionally made by partially cooking rice and vegetables separately, then layering them in a pan to finish cooking. In this quick version, they are cooked together, first on the stove top and then in the oven. Browning the sliced onions in the skillet and then layering them on top of the dish before baking adds deep flavor and textural contrast, so don't be tempted to skip this step.*

**To make the biryani**

1  In a 12-inch cast iron skillet over medium-high heat, heat the vegetable oil. Add the sliced onion and a pinch of salt, and cook, stirring frequently, until the onion becomes soft and begins to brown, about 5 minutes. Reduce the heat to medium and continue to cook, stirring occasionally, until the onions turn deep brown, about 5 to 8 minutes more. Remove the onions from the pan and set aside.

2  Add a bit more oil to the skillet, if needed, and reheat over medium-high heat. Add the garlic, jalapeño, and ginger and cook, stirring, for 30 seconds. Add the diced onion and cook, stirring, until it is soft and golden brown, about 5 minutes.

**3** Stir in the garam masala, coriander, and turmeric. Add the tomato and cook, stirring occasionally, until the tomato begins to break down, about 3 minutes. Stir in the carrots, green beans, and peas and stir to mix well.

**4** Add the rice and water and bring to a boil. Spread the charred onions over the top and transfer the skillet to the oven. Cook until the rice is tender, about 15 minutes.

### To make the raita and serve

**1** Meanwhile, in a small bowl, stir together the yogurt, cucumber, salt, and cumin.

**2** Serve the biryani hot from the oven with the raita drizzled over the top.

**ESSENTIAL TECHNIQUE:** *The charred onions add an essential layer of flavor and textural contrast to this baked rice dish, and they can do the same for other dishes, too. As long as you're taking the time to make them, double the quantity and save half for another meal. Try them on enchiladas, stuffed into wraps or burritos, or scattered over pasta dishes or salads.*

# GREEN CHILE AND SCALLION CORN PUDDING

SERVES 4 ▪ PREP TIME: 10 MINUTES ▪ COOK TIME: 45 MINUTES

1 tablespoon extra-virgin
    olive oil

2 tablespoons unsalted butter,
    divided

1 onion, halved and
    thinly sliced

1 large poblano or Anaheim
    chile, seeded and diced

2 cups fresh corn kernels
    (from about 4 ears) or
    thawed frozen corn

½ teaspoon ground cumin

¼ cup cornmeal

2 tablespoons all-purpose flour

½ teaspoon kosher salt

4 eggs, lightly beaten

1 cup milk

1 cup (4 ounces) shredded
    sharp Cheddar cheese

*Like a cross between cornbread and a savory soufflé, this creamy custard, studded with fresh corn kernels and mild green chiles, is comfort food at its finest. It makes a great simple meal served with a crisp green salad or greens sautéed with lots of garlic. Or, serve it as a side dish to accompany roasted or grilled meat, fish, or vegetables.*

1  Preheat the oven to 350°F.

2  In a 10-inch cast iron skillet over medium-high heat, heat the oil and 1 tablespoon of butter. Add the onion and chile and cook, stirring occasionally, until the onion is soft and starts to brown, about 5 minutes. Add the corn and cumin and cook, stirring, for 3 minutes. Remove the skillet from the heat.

3  In a medium bowl, stir together the cornmeal, flour, and salt. Whisk in the eggs, milk, and cheese.

4  Push the corn mixture to one side of the skillet. Add the remaining 1 tablespoon of butter to the skillet, and heat over medium heat until the butter melts. Stir to coat the skillet. Spread the corn mixture back out over the bottom. Stir the egg mixture into the corn mixture in the skillet, and spread into an even layer.

5  Transfer the skillet to the oven and bake until the center is set and a tester inserted into the center comes out clean, 30 to 35 minutes.

6  Serve warm.

# WHITE BEAN PANADE WITH TOMATOES AND KALE

SERVES 4 ▪ PREP TIME: 10 MINUTES ▪ COOK TIME: 45 MINUTES

1 tablespoon extra-virgin olive oil

1 onion, diced

3 garlic cloves, minced

8 ounces kale, ribs removed, leaves julienned

¾ teaspoon kosher salt

1 (28-ounce) can diced tomatoes with their juice

1 cup vegetable broth

1 tablespoon minced fresh oregano or 1 teaspoon crumbled dried oregano

Pinch red pepper flakes

4 thick slices of day-old bread, cut into 2-inch cubes

1 (16-ounce) can cannellini beans, drained and rinsed

1 cup shredded Parmesan or Gruyère cheese, plus more for garnish

*Reduced to its parts, this soup doesn't sound like it would add up to very much. After all, it's just stale bread, vegetables, broth, and cheese. The finished dish by far transcends the sum of its parts, however. The bread soaks up the liquid and turns into a savory, custardy bread pudding loaded with onions, greens, and tomatoes. Topped with cheese and baked until bubbly and golden brown, it's hearty, satisfying, and very delicious.*

1  Preheat the oven to 400°F.

2  In a 12-inch cast iron skillet over medium heat, heat the olive oil. Add the onion and cook, stirring frequently, until soft and translucent, about 5 minutes. Stir in the garlic and cook, stirring, for 1 minute. Add the kale and salt and cook, stirring occasionally, until tender, about 5 more minutes.

3  Increase the heat to high and add the tomatoes and their juice and the broth, oregano, and red pepper flakes. Bring to a boil, then reduce the heat to medium-low and simmer for 10 minutes.

4  Stir in the bread cubes and beans, and simmer until the bread has soaked up most of the liquid, about 5 minutes more. Remove from the heat and sprinkle the cheese evenly over the top.

5  Transfer the skillet to the preheated oven and bake until the cheese is melted, bubbly, and golden brown, about 20 minutes.

6  Serve hot.

# MAC AND CHEESE WITH CRISPY GARLIC-HERB BREAD CRUMB TOPPING

SERVES 4 ▪ PREP TIME: 15 MINUTES ▪ COOK TIME: 15 MINUTES

1 tablespoon butter,
  plus 4 tablespoons melted

1½ cups milk

1 teaspoon dry mustard

½ teaspoon ground paprika

½ teaspoon kosher salt

2½ cups (about 10 ounces)
  grated cheese(s) of
  your choice, divided

4 to 5 tablespoons
  all-purpose flour

1 (12-ounce) package
  macaroni, cooked according
  to package directions and
  kept warm

1½ cups panko bread crumbs

2 garlic cloves, minced

2 tablespoons minced
  fresh oregano

*So there's an extra pot in this recipe for cooking the pasta, but what kind of cast iron skillet cookbook would this be without a gooey, crispy-crusted mac and cheese recipe? You can use any type of melting cheese you like for this dish. Personally, I like one that's got lots of flavor, like sharp white Cheddar or Gruyère, but you could use your favorite or a combination of two or more cheeses.*

1  Preheat the broiler.

2  Heat a 10- or 12-inch cast iron skillet over low heat. Add the 1 tablespoon of unmelted butter. When the butter becomes foamy and begins to brown, whisk in the milk, mustard, paprika, and salt.

3  Add 2 cups of grated cheese to the skillet, about ½ cup at a time, whisking after each addition. When the cheese has completely melted, sift 4 tablespoons of flour into the sauce, 1 tablespoon at a time, whisking after each addition. The sauce should be thick enough to stick to the pasta. If it is too thin, whisk in the remaining 1 tablespoon of flour.

4  Add the cooked pasta to the sauce, stirring to coat well, and remove the skillet from the heat.

5  In a medium bowl, thoroughly combine the remaining ½ cup of cheese with the bread crumbs, melted butter, garlic, and oregano. Sprinkle the mixture evenly over the top of the pasta.

6  Put the skillet under the broiler and cook until the top is browned and bubbly, about 5 minutes, watching carefully so that it doesn't burn.

7  Serve hot.

# MASALA-SPICED SWEET POTATO, CHARD, AND CHICKPEAS

SERVES 4 ▪ PREP TIME: 10 MINUTES ▪ COOK TIME: 25 MINUTES

1 tablespoon coconut or extra-virgin olive oil

1½ teaspoons cumin seeds

1 yellow onion, chopped

1 green serrano pepper, seeded and minced

1 tablespoon pressed or minced fresh garlic (about 5 cloves)

1 tablespoon peeled and minced fresh ginger (about a 1-inch piece)

1½ teaspoons ground coriander

1½ teaspoons garam masala

¾ teaspoon fine sea salt

½ teaspoon ground turmeric

¼ teaspoon ground cayenne pepper (optional)

1 large sweet potato, peeled and diced small

10 to 12 leaves Swiss chard, ribs removed, leaves julienned

1 (28-ounce) can diced tomatoes with their juice

1 (14-ounce) can chickpeas (or 1½ cups cooked chickpeas), drained and rinsed

1 lemon, cut into wedges

Chopped fresh cilantro, for garnish (optional)

*Garam masala is a mixture of warm spices—usually a combination of black and white peppercorns, cloves, cinnamon, nutmeg, mace, black and green cardamom, bay leaves, and cumin—that is used in the cuisines of India and Pakistan. Here it flavors a hearty stew of greens, sweet potato, and chickpeas for a filling one-skillet meal. All you need to round it out is some warm naan (try the Onion Naan on page 156) or flat bread, or a scoop of basmati rice.*

1 In a 12-inch cast iron skillet over medium heat, heat the oil. When the oil is very hot and begins to shimmer, reduce the heat to medium-low, add the cumin seeds, and cook, stirring, until fragrant and golden brown, about 1 minute.

2 Increase the heat to medium and add the onion, serrano pepper, garlic, and ginger. Cook, stirring frequently, until the onion is soft and translucent, about 5 minutes. Add the coriander, garam masala, salt, turmeric, and cayenne (if using), and stir to mix well. Continue to cook, stirring, for 2 minutes more.

3 Add the sweet potato and chard and cook, stirring, until the chard begins to wilt, about 2 minutes. Add the tomatoes and their juice and stir to mix.

4 Increase the heat to medium-high, stir in the chickpeas, and bring to a boil. Reduce the heat to medium and simmer until the sweet potatoes are tender, about 15 minutes.

5 Serve hot, garnished with lemon wedges and cilantro (if using).

# HOISIN EGGPLANT WITH GREEN BEANS AND TOFU

SERVES 4 ▪ PREP TIME: 10 MINUTES ▪ COOK TIME: 20 MINUTES

¼ cup hoisin sauce

3 tablespoons lower-sodium soy sauce

1 tablespoon sesame oil

1 tablespoon rice vinegar

5 tablespoons vegetable oil, divided

1 (14-ounce) package firm tofu, drained and cut into cubes

2 small eggplants, cut into small chunks

8 ounces green beans, cut into 1½-inch pieces

3 garlic cloves, minced

3 scallions, white and light green parts only, thinly sliced

1 tablespoon minced fresh ginger (about a 1-inch piece)

1 tablespoon cornstarch whisked with 3 tablespoons water

Toasted sesame seeds, for garnish

*Hoisin sauce is a thick, sweet-savory mixture of soybeans, sugar, vinegar, garlic, and spices that's similar to a barbecue sauce. Here it blankets cubes of eggplant and tofu, giving them the heartiness of the meatiest barbecue, but without any meat at all.*

1  In a small bowl, combine the hoisin sauce, soy sauce, sesame oil, and rice vinegar, and stir well.

2  In a 12-inch cast iron skillet over high heat, heat 2 tablespoons of vegetable oil. Add the tofu and cook, turning occasionally, until browned, about 10 minutes. Transfer the tofu to a large bowl and set aside.

3  In the skillet over high heat, heat 2 tablespoons of the remaining oil and add the eggplant and green beans. Cook, stirring, until they are softened and beginning to brown, 6 to 8 minutes. Transfer to the bowl with the tofu.

4  In the skillet over high heat, heat the remaining 1 tablespoon of oil. Add the garlic, scallions, and ginger and stir until fragrant, about 30 seconds. Return the eggplant-tofu mixture to the pan. Add the hoisin mixture and stir to coat the vegetables and tofu well.

5  Add the cornstarch mixture to the skillet and cook, stirring, until the sauce thickens, about 1 minute more.

6  Serve hot, garnished with sesame seeds.

SEASONAL SWAP: *If eggplant is out of season, substitute peeled and diced squash like butternut or kabocha. In the summer, zucchini would work well.*

# SHAKSHUKA (NORTH AFRICAN EGGS POACHED IN SPICY TOMATO SAUCE)

SERVES 4 ▪ PREP TIME: 10 MINUTES ▪ COOK TIME: 20 MINUTES

2 tablespoons extra-virgin
    olive oil

2 onions, diced

6 garlic cloves,
    crushed and thinly sliced

1 tablespoon ground paprika

2 teaspoons ground cumin

4 large ripe tomatoes,
    diced, with their juice

2 red bell peppers,
    seeded and diced

1 to 2 jalapeño peppers,
    seeded and diced

1 tablespoon tomato paste

1 dried bay leaf

1 teaspoon kosher salt

4 eggs

Shakshuka, *a dish popular throughout the Middle East and North Africa, consists of eggs poached in a spicy tomato sauce served with crusty bread for scooping. It is frequently served as both a hearty breakfast and a quick dinner. This spicy version is based on a recipe from a Tunisian friend. She adds a generous spoonful of spicy harissa, a hot chili paste, to the sauce, which I highly recommend if you happen to have harissa in your kitchen.*

1 Preheat the oven to 400°F.

2 In a 10-inch cast iron skillet over medium-high heat, heat the olive oil. Add the onions and garlic and cook, stirring, until softened, about 4 minutes. Stir in the paprika and cumin. Add the tomatoes with their juice, bell peppers, jalapeños, tomato paste, bay leaf, and salt. Stir to mix, and bring the mixture to a boil. Cook, stirring occasionally, until the mixture thickens, about 5 minutes.

3 Make four wells in the sauce and crack an egg into each. Transfer the skillet to the oven and bake until the egg whites are set and the yolks are still a bit runny, about 12 minutes.

4 Spoon the saucy vegetable mixture onto serving plates, along with one egg per person, and serve immediately.

SEASONAL SWAP: *If good, ripe tomatoes aren't available, substitute 1 (28-ounce) can of diced tomatoes with their juice.*

# PAD SEE EW WITH CHINESE BROCCOLI, TOFU, AND EGG

SERVES 4 ▪ PREP TIME: 10 MINUTES ▪ COOK TIME: 10 MINUTES

3 tablespoons vegetarian oyster sauce

3 tablespoons dark soy sauce

3 tablespoons water

1 tablespoon lower-sodium soy sauce

1 tablespoon rice vinegar

1 tablespoon sugar

2 tablespoons vegetable oil

2 garlic cloves, minced

1 (14-ounce) package firm tofu, drained and cut into cubes

4 cups (packed) Chinese broccoli, leaves and stems separated, stems cut into strips

1 large egg

12 ounces wide rice stick noodles, soaked or boiled according to package directions, then drained

*Pad see ew, a popular street food in Thailand, means "noodles stir-fried with soy sauce" in Thai. Street vendors cook it in individual batches in only a few minutes in carts outfitted with woks. The noodles, dark soy sauce, and vegetarian oyster sauce can all be found in the Asian foods aisle of many supermarkets, Asian groceries, or online. Hoisin sauce can also be substituted for the dark soy sauce.*

1 In a small bowl, stir together the oyster sauce, dark soy sauce, and water. Add the soy sauce, vinegar, and sugar, and stir to combine.

2 In a 12-inch cast iron skillet over high heat, heat the vegetable oil. Add the garlic and cook, stirring, until fragrant, about 30 seconds. Add the tofu and broccoli stems and cook, stirring, for 3 minutes.

3 Push the broccoli stems and tofu aside and crack the egg into the skillet. Using a spatula, break the yolk and scramble the egg as it cooks. Cook until the egg is set, 1 to 2 minutes.

4 Add the noodles, broccoli leaves, and the dark soy sauce mixture and stir gently to mix, ensuring the sauce evenly coats the noodles. Cook, stirring, until the sauce is hot and thickens a bit, about 2 minutes.

5 Serve hot.

SEASONAL SWAP: *If you can't find Chinese broccoli, substitute broccoli rabe or another leafy green Chinese vegetable, like bok choy.*

# RED LENTIL AND QUINOA STEW WITH GREENS AND SAFFRON

SERVES 4 ▪ PREP TIME: 10 MINUTES ▪ COOK TIME: 20 MINUTES

2 tablespoons extra-virgin olive oil

2 carrots, diced

1 onion, diced

4 garlic cloves, minced

1 (2-inch) piece fresh ginger, peeled and minced

1½ teaspoons ground coriander

1½ teaspoons ground cumin

¾ teaspoon kosher salt

¼ teaspoon ground cayenne pepper

Pinch saffron

6 to 8 leaves kale, ribs removed, leaves julienned

1 cup red lentils

1 cup quinoa

1 cinnamon stick

4 cups vegetable broth

2 tablespoons chopped fresh cilantro

*Red lentils are one of my favorite vegetarian proteins because they're quick-cooking, delicious, and so pretty. Here they're teamed up with quinoa for even more protein. Saffron and other spices give this stew a North African vibe. It's delicious served with crusty bread for dipping. Top with a dollop of plain yogurt or sour cream if you like.*

1 In a 12-inch cast iron skillet over medium-high heat, heat the olive oil. Add the carrots and onion and cook, stirring occasionally, until the onion is soft, about 5 minutes.

2 Add the garlic, ginger, coriander, cumin, salt, cayenne, and saffron and cook, stirring, for about 30 seconds, until fragrant.

3 Add the kale, lentils, quinoa, cinnamon, and broth. Bring to a boil, reduce the heat to low, and simmer, stirring occasionally, until the quinoa and lentils are tender, about 15 minutes.

4 Remove the cinnamon stick before serving. Garnish with the cilantro.

# SPANISH TORTILLA WITH POTATOES, MANCHEGO, AND RED PEPPERS

SERVES 6 ▪ PREP TIME: 10 MINUTES ▪ COOK TIME: 35 MINUTES

3 tablespoons extra-virgin olive oil

2 pounds russet potatoes, peeled and cut into ⅛-inch slices

2 teaspoons kosher salt, divided

1 yellow onion, halved and thinly sliced

1 red bell pepper, seeded and cut into strips

8 large eggs

3 tablespoons heavy cream

1 ounce finely grated Manchego cheese (about ½ cup if grated with a microplane grater)

*Spanish tortilla, or tortilla Espanola, is a classic Spanish dish, often served as a tapa with drinks or as a take-along picnic lunch. Like the Italian frittata, it can be enjoyed hot, cold, or at room temperature. The classic version is made with just eggs and potatoes, but this version, loaded with onions, potatoes, peppers, and cheese, is satisfying enough to serve any time of the day.*

1 Preheat the oven to 350°F.

2 In a 12-inch cast iron skillet over medium-high heat, heat the olive oil. Add the potatoes and 1 teaspoon of salt. Cook, stirring occasionally, until the edges of the potatoes become translucent, about 6 minutes. Add the onion and pepper and cook, stirring, for 1 minute. Reduce the heat to medium and continue to cook, stirring occasionally, until the potatoes are tender and beginning to brown, about 7 minutes.

3 In a large bowl, whisk together the eggs, cream, and the remaining 1 teaspoon of salt.

4 Spread the vegetables out in an even layer in the skillet and pour in the egg mixture. Sprinkle the grated cheese on top, and cook just until the eggs begin to set around the edges, about 2 minutes.

5 With a rubber spatula, push the eggs away from the edge of the skillet and tilt the pan so that the raw egg runs underneath the set egg. Cook for 2 to 3 minutes more, then transfer the skillet to the preheated oven. Cook until the eggs are fully set in the middle, 10 to 15 minutes.

6 Remove from the oven and let cool for a few minutes. Slice into wedges and serve.

# ONE-PAN PASTA BAKE WITH TOMATOES, BASIL, AND RICOTTA CHEESE

SERVES 4 ▪ PREP TIME: 10 MINUTES ▪ COOK TIME: 30 MINUTES

2 tablespoons extra-virgin olive oil

2 garlic cloves, minced

1 (28-ounce) can diced tomatoes with their juice

1 (14-ounce) can tomato sauce

1 teaspoon kosher salt

Freshly ground black pepper

1 cup water, if needed

12 ounces rotini or penne pasta

1 cup ricotta cheese

½ cup freshly grated Parmesan cheese, plus more for garnish

3 tablespoons chopped fresh basil

**SEASONAL SWAP:**

*In the summertime, use 2 pounds of peeled fresh tomatoes, with their juice, instead of the canned tomatoes and sauce.*

*Make a quick tomato sauce in the skillet, add the pasta, and let it cook directly in the sauce. Top it with cheese and bake until the top is bubbly and golden brown, and you have a quick, easy dinner the whole family will love. This dish is easy to customize to your own taste, too. Add cured olives, chopped spinach, diced peppers, chickpeas, or vegetarian sausage if you like.*

1 Preheat the oven to 400°F.

2 In a 12-inch cast iron skillet over medium heat, heat the olive oil. Add the garlic and cook, stirring, until the garlic just begins to brown, about 2 minutes. Stir in the tomatoes and their juice and the tomato sauce, salt, and pepper. Increase the heat to high and cook, stirring frequently, for 5 minutes. If the sauce is very thick, add about 1 cup of water.

3 Add the pasta to the sauce, stirring to coat well. Spread the pasta out evenly, then top with evenly spaced dollops of the ricotta cheese. Sprinkle the Parmesan over the top.

4 Transfer the skillet to the oven. Bake until the pasta is tender and the cheese is bubbly and golden brown, about 20 minutes.

5 Serve hot, garnished with additional Parmesan and the fresh basil.

# FISH & SEAFOOD

## WEEKNIGHT MEALS

# LEMONY BRAISED COD WITH POTATOES, FENNEL, AND OLIVES

SERVES 4 ▪ PREP TIME: 10 MINUTES ▪ COOK TIME: 25 MINUTES

1 tablespoon extra-virgin olive oil

1 onion, thinly sliced

1 fennel bulb, thinly sliced

2 medium Yukon Gold potatoes, thinly sliced

¾ cup dry white wine

Zest and juice of 1 lemon

¾ teaspoon kosher salt, plus more for seasoning

1 cup pitted green olives, quartered lengthwise

Freshly ground black pepper

1 pound cod fillets

2 tablespoons minced fresh flat-leaf parsley

*Cod is perfect for this type of oven braising because it becomes nice and flaky while still remaining firm, plus its mild flavor plays well with the strong flavors of olives and fennel. I rarely have leftovers of this dish, but if I did, I'd chop everything into small pieces, add an egg, and make cod cakes, browning them in a little olive oil in a hot skillet for a quick, satisfying meal the next day.*

1 Preheat the oven to 450°F.

2 In a 12-inch cast iron skillet over medium-high heat, heat the olive oil. Add the onion and cook, stirring frequently, until the onion begins to soften, about 3 minutes. Add the fennel and potatoes and cook for 2 minutes more.

3 Add the wine, lemon zest, lemon juice, and salt. Bring to a boil, reduce the heat to medium-low, and simmer until the potatoes and fennel are almost tender, 8 to 10 minutes. Stir in the olives.

4 Season the fish fillets with salt and pepper, and place them on top of the vegetables, nestling them down into the liquid. Transfer the skillet to the oven and bake until the fish is just cooked through, about 10 minutes.

5 Serve the fish and vegetables immediately, garnished with the parsley.

# MAPLE PECAN–GLAZED SALMON OVER ARUGULA SALAD

SERVES 4 ▪ PREP TIME: 5 MINUTES ▪ COOK TIME: 15 MINUTES

½ cup maple syrup

3 tablespoons lower-sodium soy sauce

1 teaspoon Dijon mustard

2 tablespoons extra-virgin olive oil, divided

4 (5- to 6-ounce) salmon fillets

½ cup chopped pecans

2 tablespoons apple cider vinegar

5 ounces baby arugula

**ESSENTIAL TECHNIQUE:**

*Searing the salmon skin before baking the whole dish in the oven ensures that it gets browned and crisp. If you are using wild salmon, rather than farmed, reduce the baking time to about 8 minutes. Wild salmon is leaner than farmed and dries out easily if cooked too long.*

*Meaty salmon, sweet maple syrup, toasty pecans, and peppery arugula come together in a simple yet elegant dish that you can have on the table in minutes. This simple recipe has only a few ingredients, but the end result is surprisingly delicious. Some crusty bread or steamed brown rice would round out the meal nicely.*

1 Preheat the oven to 425°F.

2 In a small bowl, stir together the maple syrup, soy sauce, and mustard.

3 In a 12-inch cast iron skillet over medium-high heat, heat 1 tablespoon of olive oil. When the oil begins to shimmer, add the salmon, skin-side down, and cook until the skin begins to brown, about 2 minutes.

4 Spoon some of the sauce mixture over each fillet, reserving ¼ cup of the mixture for the dressing, and sprinkle the pecans evenly over the fish. Transfer the skillet to the preheated oven and bake until the fish is cooked through and flakes easily, 12 to 14 minutes.

5 Meanwhile, add the apple cider vinegar and the remaining 1 tablespoon of oil to the reserved sauce mixture, and whisk to combine. In a medium bowl, toss the arugula with the dressing.

6 To serve, divide the arugula evenly among 4 serving plates and top each with a fish fillet.

# BLACKENED FISH TACOS WITH CILANTRO-LIME CREAM

SERVES 4 ▪ PREP TIME: 10 MINUTES ▪ COOK TIME: 10 MINUTES

8 (6-inch) corn tortillas

¼ cup sour cream

2 tablespoons minced fresh cilantro

2 tablespoons freshly squeezed lime juice

1 jalapeño pepper, seeded and finely minced

1½ teaspoons ground paprika

1½ teaspoons brown sugar

1 teaspoon dried oregano

¾ teaspoon garlic powder

½ teaspoon ground cumin

½ teaspoon kosher salt

¼ teaspoon ground cayenne pepper

4 (6-ounce) tilapia fillets

1 tablespoon vegetable oil

½ ripe peeled avocado, thinly sliced

2 cups thinly shredded cabbage

1 lime, cut into 4 wedges

*Who doesn't love taco night? Feel free to replace the avocado slices with guacamole, or add thinly sliced radishes, grilled scallions, or a homemade or store-bought pico de gallo and a side of chips.*

1 Preheat the oven to 450°F.

2 Wrap the tortillas in aluminum foil and heat in the oven while you prepare the rest of the dish.

3 In a small bowl, stir together the sour cream, cilantro, lime juice, and jalapeño.

4 In another small bowl, mix together the paprika, brown sugar, oregano, garlic powder, cumin, salt, and cayenne. Sprinkle the spice mixture evenly over the fish, coating both sides of each fillet.

5 In a 12-inch cast iron skillet over medium-high heat, heat the vegetable oil. When the oil begins to shimmer, add the fish and cook until cooked through and lightly browned, about 3 minutes per side.

6 Remove the tortillas from the oven and place two on each serving plate, overlapping. Place a fish fillet on top of each stack of tortillas and drizzle the cilantro-lime cream over the top. Divide the avocado slices evenly among the tacos and top each with a handful of shredded cabbage. Serve immediately with lime wedges on the side.

**PERFECT PAIRING:** *If you want a dish that will knock your guests off their feet, serve these with Homemade Corn Tortillas (page 154).*

# SKILLET-ROASTED MAHIMAHI WITH POTATOES, GREEN OLIVES, AND CAPERS

SERVES 4 ▪ PREP TIME: 10 MINUTES ▪ COOK TIME: 30 MINUTES

4 tablespoons extra-virgin
   olive oil, divided

6 canned plum tomatoes,
   drained and coarsely
   chopped

2 celery stalks, diced

½ red onion, halved and sliced

1 cup pitted green olives

¼ cup capers,
   plus more for garnish

1 garlic clove, minced

⅛ teaspoon red pepper flakes,
   or to taste

1½ cups peeled and thinly
   sliced yellow-fleshed
   potatoes

Kosher salt

Freshly ground black pepper

1¼ pounds mahimahi fillets
   (about ¾-inch thick)

¼ cup chopped fresh
   flat-leaf parsley

*Mahimahi is a firm-fleshed, meaty fish that takes especially well to oven roasting. Green olives, capers, red onions, and tomatoes infuse it with tons of flavor, and the potatoes make it a satisfying one-skillet meal.*

1 Preheat the oven to 400°F.

2 In a 12-inch cast iron skillet, swirl 3 tablespoons of olive oil to coat the bottom of the pan. Add the tomatoes, celery, onion, olives, capers, garlic, and red pepper flakes to the skillet and toss to combine. Arrange the potato slices on top of the vegetables, and season with salt and pepper.

3 Cover the skillet with aluminum foil and set over medium-low heat. Let it simmer, without stirring, until the potatoes begin to soften, about 20 minutes.

4 Pat the fish dry with paper towels and season both sides with salt and pepper.

5 Remove the foil from the skillet and lay the fish fillets on top of the potatoes. Drizzle the remaining 1 tablespoon of oil over the fish. Transfer the skillet to the oven and cook until the fish is cooked through, about 8 minutes.

6 Serve hot, garnished with the parsley and more capers.

**ESSENTIAL TECHNIQUE:** *Roasting is an easy way to cook fish without drying it out. Most fish should be roasted for about 10 minutes per inch of thickness (measured at the thickest point.)*

# MASALA SEA BASS

SERVES 4 ▪ PREP TIME: 10 MINUTES ▪ COOK TIME: 15 MINUTES

2 tablespoons coconut or vegetable oil

2 teaspoons black mustard seeds

5 (⅛-inch-thick) slices peeled fresh ginger, smashed

2 large garlic cloves, smashed

1 or 2 (2-inch) fresh hot green chiles such as Thai or serrano, halved lengthwise

2 tablespoons ground coriander

1 teaspoon Indian chili powder

½ teaspoon ground turmeric

½ teaspoon curry powder

3 medium tomatoes, coarsely chopped

¾ cup water

¼ cup coconut cream

2 pounds sea bass fillets, with skin, cut into 1-inch cubes

¾ teaspoon kosher salt

5 ounces baby spinach

*This fish curry is quick to prepare and makes a really satisfying and healthy meal. I love it with a side of plain naan that I use to sop up the flavorful sauce. Change up this dish by using different types of fish (cod, halibut, or tilapia would all be great choices) or adding different vegetables, like bell peppers or peas.*

1 In a 12-inch cast iron skillet over medium-high heat, heat the oil. When the oil begins to shimmer, add the mustard seeds and cook until they begin to pop, about 15 seconds.

2 Stir in the ginger, garlic, and chiles and cook, stirring, for 1 minute. Add the coriander, chili powder, turmeric, and curry powder and stir to mix. Add the tomatoes and cook, stirring, until the tomatoes are heated through, about 1 minute.

3 Add the water and bring to a boil. Reduce the heat to low and simmer for 5 minutes. Stir in the coconut cream, fish, and salt. Continue to simmer until the fish is just cooked through, 3 to 5 minutes.

4 Add the spinach and cook, stirring gently, until the spinach is wilted, about 2 minutes. Serve immediately.

DID YOU KNOW? *Coconut cream is the thick cream that separates out from full-fat coconut milk. You can often find coconut cream in cans in many supermarkets or Asian markets, or you can use the cream from a can of coconut milk. Chill a can of full-fat coconut milk in the refrigerator. Open the can carefully and scoop off the layer of thick cream from the top. Reserve the remaining liquid for another use.*

# SHRIMP WITH BLISTERED CHERRY TOMATOES, ORZO, FETA, AND FRESH MINT

SERVES 4 ▪ PREP TIME: 10 MINUTES ▪ COOK TIME: 20 MINUTES

2 tablespoons, plus 1 teaspoon extra-virgin olive oil, divided

6 garlic cloves, minced

3 cups halved cherry tomatoes (about 1 pound)

12 ounces dried orzo

3¼ cups chicken or vegetable broth

¾ teaspoon kosher salt, divided

1 pound peeled and deveined large shrimp

Freshly ground black pepper

1 cup crumbled feta cheese

1 cup fresh mint leaves, torn

*This pasta dinner is perfect for a summer evening since it's best when tomatoes are at their peak. Mint adds a bright, herbal, and slightly unexpected flavor note to the dish, but you could substitute basil if you like. Orzo is small, rice-shaped pasta that cooks quickly, making it perfect for this in-sauce cooking technique.*

1 Preheat the oven to 400°F.

2 In a 12-inch cast iron skillet over medium heat, heat 2 tablespoons of olive oil. Add the garlic and cook, stirring, until it begins to brown, about 1 minute. Increase the heat to high and add the tomatoes. Cook, stirring occasionally, until the tomatoes begin to blister and break down a bit, about 5 minutes.

3 Stir in the orzo, broth, and ½ teaspoon of salt, and bring to a simmer. Remove from the heat, cover the skillet with aluminum foil, and transfer to the oven. Bake until the orzo is tender and the liquid has mostly been absorbed, about 10 minutes. Remove the skillet from the oven, and turn the broiler on.

4 Meanwhile, in a medium bowl, toss the shrimp with the remaining 1 teaspoon of oil and the remaining ¼ teaspoon of salt, and season with pepper.

5 Remove the foil from the skillet and arrange the shrimp on top of the pasta mixture. Sprinkle the cheese over the top. Heat under the broiler until the shrimp are cooked through and the cheese is melted and beginning to brown, about 4 minutes.

6 Sprinkle with the mint and serve immediately.

# MUSSELS STEAMED IN LEMONGRASS-COCONUT BROTH

SERVES 4 ▪ PREP TIME: 10 MINUTES ▪ COOK TIME: 10 MINUTES

1 cup bottled clam juice

1 cup unsweetened
coconut milk

Finely grated zest of 1 lime

1½ teaspoons rice vinegar

1½ teaspoons sugar

¼ teaspoon kosher salt

2 tablespoons extra-virgin
olive oil

½ teaspoon sesame oil

1 stalk fresh lemongrass,
white part only,
finely grated

1 garlic clove, minced

1 (1-inch) piece fresh ginger,
peeled and minced

1 tablespoon chopped scallion
(green parts only)

1 tablespoon chopped shallot

½ teaspoon red pepper flakes

2 pounds live mussels in their
shells, scrubbed and rinsed

½ cup coarsely chopped
fresh cilantro

*Mussels are far too often overlooked as a simple and delicious meal option. They are inexpensive, quick and easy to cook, and taste divine. This Thai-inspired broth is flavored with coconut milk, lemongrass, garlic, ginger, and red pepper, infusing the sweet, plump mussels with intense spicy-sweet flavor. The broth is so good, you may forgo your spoon to dunk in hunks of crusty bread instead.*

1  In a medium bowl, stir together the clam juice, coconut milk, lime zest, vinegar, sugar, and salt.

2  In a 12-inch cast iron skillet over medium-high heat, heat the olive and sesame oils. When the oil begins to shimmer, add the lemongrass, garlic, ginger, scallion, shallot, and red pepper flakes and cook, stirring, just until fragrant, about 15 seconds. Add the clam juice mixture and bring to a boil. Add the mussels and stir to coat. Cover the skillet and cook until most of the mussels open (discard any mussels that don't open), about 5 minutes.

3  Remove the cover, stir in the cilantro, and serve immediately.

**ESSENTIAL TECHNIQUE:** *The mussels are cooked by steaming them in the broth mixture. If you don't have a lid for your skillet, use a large lid from another skillet or pot. If you don't have a large enough lid, use a piece of aluminum foil. Press the foil on with oven mitt–protected hands.*

# SPICY KUNG PAO PRAWNS

SERVES 4 ▪ PREP TIME: 10 MINUTES ▪ COOK TIME: 10 MINUTES

## FOR THE SAUCE

¼ cup low-sodium soy sauce

¼ cup sweet soy sauce

¼ cup water

1 teaspoon rice vinegar

1 teaspoon sesame oil

1 teaspoon cornstarch

1 teaspoon sugar

½ teaspoon white pepper

## FOR THE SHRIMP

2 tablespoons vegetable oil

1 (2-inch) piece ginger, peeled and thinly sliced

½ onion, thinly sliced

1 green bell pepper, seeded and diced

5 to 10 small dried red chiles

1¼ pounds peeled and deveined large shrimp

½ cup roasted peanuts

4 scallions, white and light green parts only, thinly sliced

*This quick home version of a favorite Chinese restaurant dish is so easy and so tasty, you'll swear you're never going to order takeout again. The high heat of the cast iron skillet toasts the chiles, infusing the oil with smoky spice. If you can buy your shrimp already peeled and deveined, the prep will go even quicker.*

**To make the sauce**

In a small bowl, stir well to mix the soy sauce, sweet soy sauce, water, vinegar, sesame oil, cornstarch, sugar, and white pepper.

**To cook the shrimp**

1 In a 12-inch cast iron skillet over high heat, heat the vegetable oil. When the oil begins to shimmer, add the ginger and stir. Add the onion, bell pepper, and chiles. Cook, stirring, until you begin to smell the spiciness of the chiles, about 1 minute. Add the shrimp and peanuts and continue to cook, stirring frequently, until the shrimp are cooked through, about 4 minutes.

2 Stir in the sauce mixture and cook, stirring, until the sauce thickens, another 2 to 3 minutes.

3 Stir in the scallions and serve immediately.

# SEARED DAY BOAT SCALLOPS WITH LEMON, BACON, AND FRESH PEAS

SERVES 4 ▪ PREP TIME: 10 MINUTES ▪ COOK TIME: 20 MINUTES

4 slices thick-cut bacon, cut into ¼-inch matchsticks

3 tablespoons unsalted butter, divided

16 large sea scallops (about 1½ pounds)

Kosher salt

Freshly ground black pepper

½ small Vidalia or other sweet onion, cut into ½-inch pieces

2 cups fresh or frozen (thawed) peas

¼ cup chicken broth

1 teaspoon freshly squeezed lemon juice

2 tablespoons finely chopped fresh flat-leaf parsley

*Scallops are another seafood that is surprisingly easy to cook. The trick is to cook them in a very hot skillet so that they brown quickly without overcooking. For this reason, a cast iron skillet is the ideal cooking vessel. Peas, bacon, and lemon are all perfect partners for the sweet, meaty scallops.*

1  Heat a 12-inch cast iron skillet over medium heat. Add the bacon and cook, stirring frequently, until crisp and browned, about 4 minutes. Use a slotted spoon to transfer the bacon to a paper towel–lined plate.

2  Discard all but 1 tablespoon of bacon fat from the skillet, and add 1 tablespoon of butter. Heat the pan over medium-high heat until the butter is melted.

3  Meanwhile, pat the scallops very dry with paper towels and season them with salt and pepper. Reduce the heat to medium, add the scallops, and cook, turning once, until nicely browned and just cooked through, 5 to 6 minutes. Transfer the scallops to a plate.

4  Add the remaining 2 tablespoons of butter to the skillet and melt. Add the onion and cook, stirring frequently, until it is soft, about 5 minutes. Stir in the peas and broth and cook until just heated through, 2 to 3 minutes. Stir in the lemon juice, parsley, reserved bacon, and the scallops, and cook another minute or so, until heated through.

5  Season with salt and pepper and serve hot.

# POULTRY

## WEEKNIGHT MEALS

# PAN-ROASTED LEMON CHICKEN DRUMSTICKS WITH POTATOES AND LEEKS

SERVES 4 TO 6 ▪ PREP TIME: 5 MINUTES ▪ COOK TIME: 50 MINUTES

2 tablespoons extra-virgin olive oil

3 medium lemons, sliced into rounds (with the peel left intact)

8 skin-on chicken drumsticks

½ teaspoon kosher salt, plus more for seasoning

Freshly ground black pepper

1 pound baby Yukon Gold potatoes, cut in half

2 leeks, white and light green parts only, sliced

Juice of 2 lemons

½ cup dry white wine

10 cherry tomatoes

*This one-pan chicken dinner has a delightfully short ingredient list, but it is long on flavor. The bright yellow lemons, Yukon gold potatoes, leeks, cherry tomatoes, and chicken make for a beautiful presentation, too. If you want to temper the bitterness of the lemon peels, blanch the 3 whole lemons in boiling water for a few minutes before slicing them.*

1  Preheat the oven to 450°F.

2  In a 14-inch cast iron skillet over medium heat, heat the olive oil. Add the lemon slices and cook until they brown on the bottom, about 4 minutes. Transfer the lemon slices to a plate and set aside.

3  Increase the heat to medium-high. Season the chicken on all sides with salt and pepper. Place the chicken in the hot pan, skin-side down. Cook until the skin is golden brown, 3 to 4 minutes. Turn the chicken over and cook until the second side is browned, 3 to 4 minutes more.

4  Place the potatoes and leeks around the chicken. Layer the lemon slices over the chicken pieces in the pan. Sprinkle the remaining ½ teaspoon of salt and some pepper over the top, and add the lemon juice and wine to the pan. Transfer the skillet to the oven and bake for 20 minutes. Add the cherry tomatoes and bake for another 10-15 minutes, until the chicken is cooked through.

5  Serve warm.

# SKILLET-ROASTED CHICKEN WITH PANCETTA AND ASPARAGUS

SERVES 4 ▪ PREP TIME: 10 MINUTES ▪ COOK TIME: 45 MINUTES

4 (⅛-inch-thick) slices pancetta, diced

8 bone-in, skin-on chicken thighs

Kosher salt

Freshly ground black pepper

2 medium shallots, thinly sliced

1 pound asparagus spears, trimmed

½ cup dry white wine

1½ cups chicken broth

2 tablespoons all-purpose flour

1 teaspoon finely grated lemon zest

*This all-in-one meal includes succulent roasted asparagus and a flavorful pan sauce, and it all comes together in under an hour. It's a perfect simple meal for a busy weeknight. You can substitute regular bacon if you don't have pancetta.*

1 Preheat the oven to 425°F.

2 Heat a 12-inch cast iron skillet over medium-high heat. Add the pancetta and cook, stirring occasionally, until beginning to brown, about 4 minutes.

3 Season the chicken all over with salt and pepper and add it to the skillet, skin-side down, along with the shallots. Cook until the skin of the chicken is browned, about 3 minutes. Turn the chicken and shallots over.

4 Arrange the asparagus around the chicken and transfer the skillet to the oven. Roast until the chicken is cooked through and the asparagus is tender, about 30 minutes. Remove the skillet from the oven.

5 Transfer the chicken and vegetables to a serving platter and return the skillet to the stove top over medium-high heat. Add the wine to deglaze the pan and cook, stirring and scraping up any browned bits from the bottom of the pan, until the wine is reduced by half, about 2 minutes.

6 In a small bowl, whisk together the broth, flour, and lemon zest. Add the broth mixture to the pan and cook, stirring, until the sauce bubbles and thickens, about 5 minutes longer.

7 Pour the sauce over the chicken and vegetables on the platter and serve immediately.

**ESSENTIAL TECHNIQUE:**
*The term "deglazing" means to add liquid, usually wine or another alcoholic liquid, to a hot pan that meat has been cooked in to make a pan sauce. The liquid quickly boils and helps release the flavor-packed bits of caramelized meat and vegetables that have stuck to the bottom of the pan. Next, more liquid (such as broth) and some sort of thickening agent (like flour) are usually added, along with various seasonings.*

# CHICKEN AND SAUSAGE JAMBALAYA

SERVES 6 ▪ PREP TIME: 10 MINUTES ▪ COOK TIME: 40 MINUTES

2 tablespoons vegetable oil

1 tablespoon butter

¾ pound andouille sausage, sliced

1 pound boneless, skin-on chicken thighs

Kosher salt

Freshly ground black pepper

2 celery stalks, diced

1 large yellow onion, diced

1 large green bell pepper, seeded and diced

1 garlic clove, minced

1 teaspoon ground paprika

½ teaspoon ground cayenne pepper

2 dried bay leaves

3 cups chicken broth

1 (14-ounce) can diced tomatoes

1 tablespoon fresh thyme leaves

1½ cups long grain white rice

*Jambalaya is a classic Cajun rice stew filled with assorted meats and vegetables. Like any good Cajun recipe, it starts with the "holy trinity"—onion, bell peppers, and celery. From there the flavor is built with cayenne, fresh thyme, tomatoes, chicken, and spicy andouille sausage. Rice gets stirred into the saucy mix, and the whole thing bakes in the oven until the rice is tender.*

1  Preheat the oven to 425°F.

2  In a 12-inch cast iron skillet over medium-high heat, heat the vegetable oil and butter. Add the sausage and cook until browned on both sides, about 4 minutes. Transfer the sausage to a plate and set aside.

3  Season the chicken pieces all over with salt and pepper. Add them to the skillet, skin-side down, and cook until the skin is golden brown, about 3 minutes. Turn the chicken over and cook until the second side is browned, 2 to 3 minutes more. Transfer the chicken to the plate with the sausage.

4  Add the celery, onion, and bell pepper to the skillet and cook, stirring, until they begin to soften, about 3 minutes. Stir in the garlic and cook, stirring, for 1 minute more.

5  Add the paprika, cayenne, and bay leaves. Cook, stirring, for 1 minute, then stir in the broth, tomatoes, and thyme. Bring the liquid to a boil. Stir the rice into the mixture in the skillet and then return the sausage and chicken to the skillet, distributing them evenly over the top.

6  Transfer the skillet to the oven and bake until the rice is tender, the chicken is cooked through, and the liquid has been absorbed, 20 to 25 minutes.

7  Remove and discard the bay leaves and serve immediately.

# CHICKEN IN MUSHROOM CREAM SAUCE

SERVES 4 ▪ PREP TIME: 10 MINUTES ▪ COOK TIME: 50 MINUTES

3 tablespoons extra-virgin olive oil, divided

8 boneless, skin-on chicken thighs

12 ounces cremini or button mushrooms, sliced

½ onion, diced

¾ cup dry white wine

1½ cups chicken broth

¾ cup heavy cream

1 tablespoon plus 1½ teaspoons Dijon mustard

2 tablespoons chopped fresh tarragon leaves

*This simple but deeply satisfying chicken dish—rich with cream and loaded with fresh mushrooms—can be on the table in an hour. Serve it for a quick family weeknight dinner or as a special meal for guests. It's the perfect choice for either situation.*

1 In a 12-inch cast iron skillet over medium-high heat, heat 2 tablespoons of olive oil. When the oil begins to shimmer, add the chicken, skin-side down. Cook until the skin is golden brown, about 3 minutes. Turn the chicken over and cook until the second side is browned, 2 to 3 minutes more. Transfer to a plate and set aside.

2 Drain any remaining cooking fat from the skillet and add the remaining 1 tablespoon of olive oil. Heat over medium-high heat. When the oil is hot, add the mushrooms and cook, stirring occasionally, until they are browned, about 6 minutes. Add the onion and continue to cook, stirring frequently, until the onion is softened, about 3 minutes more. Stir in the wine and cook until the liquid is reduced to just a few tablespoons, about 5 minutes.

3 Add the broth, cream, and mustard and stir to combine. Bring the liquid to a boil, reduce the heat to medium, and continue to cook until the sauce is reduced by half, 6 to 8 minutes.

4 Add the chicken back to the skillet and continue cooking until the chicken is cooked through, 15 to 20 minutes more. Stir in the tarragon and cook a minute longer.

5 Serve hot.

# THAI CURRY CHICKEN WITH COCONUT MILK AND FRESH BASIL

SERVES 4 ▪ PREP TIME: 10 MINUTES ▪ COOK TIME: 20 MINUTES

3½ cups unsweetened coconut milk, divided

1 tablespoon plus 1 teaspoon Thai red curry paste

8 kaffir lime leaves or finely grated zest of 1 lime

1 large onion, thinly sliced

2 large leafy Thai basil or regular basil sprigs

1½ pounds boneless, skinless chicken breast, cut into ¼- to ⅓-inch-thick slices

1 large red bell pepper, seeded and cut into strips

1 (8-ounce) can bamboo shoots, drained

4 teaspoons tamarind paste

2 teaspoons fish sauce

1 teaspoon sugar

*This dish is so easy and so tasty that you may never want to go out for Thai food again. Thai curry paste, which can be found in most supermarkets or in Asian groceries, gives it loads of complex flavor. Rich coconut milk and fresh basil round out the flavor. Serve it over steamed white or brown rice if you like.*

1  In a 12-inch cast iron skillet over medium-high heat, combine ½ cup of coconut milk with the curry paste and kaffir lime leaves and heat, stirring occasionally, until the mixture bubbles and thickens, about 3 minutes.

2  Add the remaining 3 cups of coconut milk and the onion and basil sprigs and bring to a boil. Cook, stirring occasionally, until the mixture thickens, about 5 minutes.

3  Reduce the heat to medium-low and stir in the chicken, bell pepper, bamboo shoots, tamarind paste, fish sauce, and sugar. Simmer until the chicken is cooked through, 6 to 8 minutes.

4  Serve hot.

**DID YOU KNOW?** *Tamarind paste, a common ingredient in Thai and other Southeast Asian and South Asian cuisines, is the concentrated and deseeded fruit of the tamarind tree. You can buy the paste in tubs in some supermarkets or Asian grocery stores or online. You can also substitute lime juice in equal measure.*

# CRISPY CHICKEN THIGHS WITH HONEY-SRIRACHA GLAZE AND CABBAGE SLAW

SERVES 4 ▪ PREP TIME: 10 MINUTES, PLUS 15 TO 30 MINUTES TO MARINATE
COOK TIME: 25 MINUTES

## FOR THE CHICKEN

3 tablespoons honey

3 tablespoons rice vinegar

2 tablespoons lower-sodium soy sauce

2 teaspoons sriracha sauce

Pinch salt

4 garlic cloves, minced

8 boneless, skin-on chicken thighs

## FOR THE SLAW

2 tablespoons rice vinegar

2 tablespoons extra-virgin olive oil

¼ teaspoon kosher salt

⅛ teaspoon freshly ground black pepper

2 cups finely shredded green cabbage

2 carrots, peeled and grated on the large holes of a box grater

## FOR COOKING

2 tablespoons vegetable oil

*Combining spicy, tangy sriracha sauce with sweet honey is genius. The chicken is infused with flavor and then baked in the oven, and the marinade is cooked down to an addictive glaze. The chicken and slaw together make a nice light meal, but you might want to add rice, just to have something to drizzle more of the delicious sauce on.*

Preheat the oven to 400°F.

**To prepare the chicken**

In a large bowl, whisk together the honey, vinegar, soy sauce, sriracha, salt, and garlic. Add the chicken to the sauce mixture and stir to coat. Marinate for 15 to 30 minutes.

**To make the slaw**

In a large bowl, whisk together the vinegar, olive oil, salt, and pepper. Add the cabbage and carrot and toss to coat.

**To cook**

1 In a 12-inch cast iron skillet over medium heat, heat the vegetable oil. Remove the chicken from the marinade, reserving the marinade, and add the chicken, skin-side down, to the skillet. Cook until the skin is golden brown, about 3 minutes. Flip the chicken over and cook until the second side is browned, about 3 minutes more.

2 Transfer the skillet to the oven and bake until the chicken is cooked through, about 15 minutes.

3 Remove the skillet from the oven and place it on the stove top over medium-high heat. Add the reserved marinade to the skillet and cook until it thickens, about 5 minutes.

4 Remove the skillet from the heat and serve immediately, with the slaw on the side.

PERFECT PAIRING:
*Serve this spicy chicken dish with ice-cold beer to quench the fire.*

# CHICKEN CHILAQUILES

SERVES 4 ▪ PREP TIME: 10 MINUTES ▪ COOK TIME: 20 MINUTES

1½ pounds fresh tomatillos, husked, rinsed, and halved

2 large garlic cloves

1 large jalapeño pepper, halved lengthwise, stemmed and seeded

¼ cup packed fresh cilantro

2 tablespoons vegetable oil

1 teaspoon ground cumin

½ teaspoon ground coriander

1 teaspoon kosher salt

½ teaspoon freshly ground black pepper

1 pound (about 3 cups) shredded cooked chicken, at room temperature

1½ cups (about 6 ounces) shredded pepper Jack cheese, divided

½ cup (about 4 ounces) queso fresco

1 scallion, sliced

One 6-ounce bag tortilla chips (8 cups)

*Chilaquiles is a dish that was invented specifically as a way to use up leftovers. In Mexico, it is often made with day-old corn tortillas that are cut into strips and fried. This quicker version substitutes tortilla chips. Sure, it's a little naughty, but so satisfying after a long day at the office.*

1 Preheat the oven to 450°F.

2 In a food processor or blender, process the tomatillos, garlic, jalapeño, and cilantro until smooth.

3 In a 12-inch cast iron skillet over medium-high heat, heat the vegetable oil. When the oil begins to shimmer, add the cumin and coriander and cook, stirring, until fragrant, about 30 seconds. Add the tomatillo mixture and bring to a boil. Cook, stirring frequently, for 3 minutes. Stir in the salt and pepper.

4 In a medium bowl, toss together the chicken, ¾ cup of cheese, the queso fresco, scallion, and half of the tomatillo sauce.

5 In a large bowl, combine the tortilla chips with the rest of the sauce, tossing to coat.

6 Arrange half of the chips in the skillet in an even layer, and top with the chicken mixture. Arrange the remaining chips in an even layer on top of the chicken, and sprinkle the remaining ¾ cup of cheese over the top.

7 Transfer the skillet to the oven and bake until the cheese is melted and browned, about 15 minutes.

8 Serve immediately.

# NORTH AFRICAN CHICKEN WITH ALMONDS, CHICKPEAS, AND RAISINS

SERVES 4 ▪ PREP TIME: 5 MINUTES ▪ COOK TIME: 25 MINUTES

1 tablespoon all-purpose flour

¼ teaspoon kosher salt

¼ teaspoon freshly ground black pepper

1½ pounds boneless, skinless chicken thighs

1 tablespoon vegetable oil

1 onion, thinly sliced

1 garlic clove, minced

1 jalapeño pepper, seeded and minced

½ teaspoon ground cinnamon

½ teaspoon ground coriander

½ teaspoon ground ginger

¼ teaspoon ground allspice

¼ teaspoon ground turmeric

1 cup chicken broth

½ cup raisins

1 (14-ounce) can chickpeas, drained and rinsed

1 teaspoon red wine vinegar

2 tablespoons sliced almonds

*Succulent chicken, plump, sweet raisins, and lots of heady spices make this a winner of a chicken dinner. It may look like a long list of ingredients, but there is very little prep work involved. This dish can easily be on the table in 30 minutes.*

1 In a shallow bowl, whisk together the flour, salt, and pepper. Dredge the chicken in the flour mixture.

2 In a 12-inch cast iron skillet over medium-high heat, heat the vegetable oil. When the oil begins to shimmer, add the chicken. Cook until nicely browned, about 3 minutes. Turn over and cook until the second side is browned, about 3 minutes more. Transfer the chicken to a bowl.

3 Add the onion to the skillet and cook, stirring frequently, until softened and beginning to brown, 5 to 6 minutes. Stir in the garlic, jalapeño, cinnamon, coriander, ginger, allspice, and turmeric and cook, stirring, for 30 seconds. Stir in the broth and raisins.

4 Return the chicken to the skillet, reduce the heat to low, and simmer until the chicken is cooked through, about 10 minutes.

5 Stir in the chickpeas and cook until heated through, about 2 minutes.

6 Stir in the vinegar and serve immediately, garnished with the sliced almonds.

# CRISPY DUCK BREAST WITH BALSAMIC-FIG REDUCTION

SERVES 4 ▪ PREP TIME: 5 MINUTES ▪ COOK TIME: 30 MINUTES

## FOR THE DUCK BREASTS

2 to 3 duck breasts (about 2 pounds total)

Kosher salt

Freshly ground black pepper

1 tablespoon extra-virgin olive oil

## FOR THE BALSAMIC-FIG REDUCTION

1 shallot, minced

¾ cup dry sherry

1½ cups chicken broth

¼ cup balsamic vinegar

¼ cup fig jam

Kosher salt (if needed)

Freshly ground black pepper (if needed)

2 tablespoons unsalted butter, chilled

## FOR THE GARNISH

Chopped fresh chives

*Searing a duck breast in a very hot pan on the stove top and finishing it in the oven gives it a crispy skin and a perfectly medium-rare interior. While the duck breasts rest, you'll have just enough time to whip up a sweet-savory balsamic-fig sauce that will finish it beautifully. Serve an arugula salad or steamed green beans alongside for an easy but impressive meal.*

### To cook the duck breasts

1 Preheat the oven to 400°F.

2 On a plate, score the fatty side of the duck breasts in a crosshatch pattern, cutting through the skin and fat layer but not into the meat. Season on both sides with salt and pepper.

3 In a 12-inch cast iron skillet over medium-high heat, heat the olive oil. Add the duck breasts, skin-side down, and cook until the skin is a deep golden brown and crispy and the fat begins to render, about 5 minutes. Turn the breasts over and sear for 4 to 5 minutes on the second side, until golden brown.

4 Transfer the skillet to the oven and cook for 5 minutes more for medium-rare. Remove from the oven and transfer the duck breasts to a cutting board. Let rest for at least 5 minutes.

**To make the balsamic-fig reduction**

1 Drain all but about 2 tablespoons of the fat from the skillet. Set the skillet over medium heat, add the shallot, and cook, stirring, until softened, about 3 minutes. Add the sherry and cook until the liquid is reduced by half, about 3 minutes. Stir in the broth, vinegar, and jam and simmer until the sauce becomes thick and syrupy, 5 to 7 minutes more.

2 Remove the skillet from the heat. Taste and season with salt and pepper if needed. Whisk in the butter until it is completely incorporated into the sauce.

**To garnish and serve**

Slice the duck breasts thinly and arrange on serving plates. Drizzle the sauce over the top and garnish with chives.

# PORK & BEEF

## WEEKNIGHT MEALS

# CHINESE STIR-FRIED NOODLES WITH GROUND PORK

SERVES 4 ▪ PREP TIME: 10 MINUTES ▪ COOK TIME: 10 MINUTES

¼ cup Shaoxing wine

2 tablespoons lower-sodium soy sauce

2 tablespoons sesame oil

2 tablespoons oyster sauce

2 tablespoons cornstarch

2 teaspoons brown sugar

½ teaspoon white pepper

1 cup water

1 tablespoon vegetable oil

2 garlic cloves, minced, divided

2 tablespoons minced fresh ginger, divided

1 pound ground pork

½ head napa cabbage, thinly sliced

1 pound fresh Shanghai-style noodles or fresh fettuccini or spaghetti

*This quick Shanghai-style noodle stir-fry uses fresh noodles, which means they don't need to be precooked in boiling water. The result: You can get this complete meal on the table fast. The meat and cabbage are quickly stir-fried, along with the aromatics, and then the noodles are added along with a sauce mixture. Cornstarch thickens the sauce as it cooks, coating the noodles with intense flavor.*

1 In a small bowl, stir together the wine, soy sauce, sesame oil, oyster sauce, cornstarch, sugar, white pepper, and water to mix well.

2 In a 12-inch cast iron skillet over medium-high heat, heat the vegetable oil. Add 1 minced garlic clove and 1 tablespoon of minced ginger and cook, stirring, until they become fragrant, about 1 minute. Add the pork and cook, breaking the meat up with a spatula, until the meat is browned, about 5 minutes. Stir in the cabbage and the remaining minced garlic clove and 1 tablespoon of minced ginger and cook, stirring frequently, until the cabbage is tender, about 4 minutes more.

3 Add the noodles along with the sauce mixture and toss to combine. Bring to a boil and cook until the noodles are tender and the sauce has thickened a bit, about 2 minutes more.

4 Serve hot.

**DID YOU KNOW?** *Shaoxing wine is a Chinese rice wine often used in cooking. You can find it in the Asian foods aisle of many supermarkets or in Asian markets, or you can substitute dry sherry, sake, or any dry white wine.*

# PAN-ROASTED PORK CHOPS WITH SWEET AND SOUR BRAISED RED CABBAGE

SERVES 4 ▪ PREP TIME: 10 MINUTES ▪ COOK TIME: 45 MINUTES

6 bacon slices, chopped

1 medium onion, chopped

1 small red cabbage
(about 1¾ pounds),
halved lengthwise, cored,
and sliced ¼ inch thick

¾ cup water

¼ cup red wine vinegar

2 tablespoons sugar

½ teaspoon caraway seeds

1¼ teaspoons kosher salt,
divided

¾ teaspoon freshly ground
black pepper, divided

4 (1-inch-thick) bone-in
rib pork chops
(2½ to 3 pounds total)

2 tablespoons vegetable oil

*You begin this dish by first cooking bacon in the skillet, laying down a layer of flavor. Then you cook the cabbage and pork chops in the bacon fat. First the cabbage is braised, then the pork chops are seared and then pan-roasted in the oven. The whole dish takes less than an hour to prepare, but it tastes like the kind of meal you slave over all day.*

1 Preheat the oven to 450°F.

2 In a 12-inch cast iron skillet over medium-high heat, cook the bacon until browned and crisp, about 5 minutes. Transfer to a paper towel–lined plate to drain.

3 With the skillet still over medium-high heat, add the onion and cook, stirring occasionally, until it softens and begins to turn brown, about 3 minutes. Add the cabbage and toss until it is coated with the fat. Stir in the water, vinegar, sugar, caraway seeds, ¾ teaspoon of salt, and ¼ teaspoon of pepper.

4 Reduce the heat to medium-low and braise the cabbage, stirring occasionally, for about 25 minutes, until the cabbage is tender. Transfer the cabbage to a serving platter and wipe out the skillet.

5  Season the pork chops with the remaining ½ teaspoon of salt and ½ teaspoon of pepper. In the skillet over medium-high heat, heat the vegetable oil. When the oil begins to shimmer, add the chops and cook until golden brown on the bottom, about 3 minutes. Flip over and cook until the second side is browned, about 3 minutes more. Transfer the skillet to the preheated oven and roast the chops until they are cooked through, 5 to 7 minutes.

6  While the pork is cooking, stir half of the cooked bacon into the cabbage. Run a knife through the remaining bacon to chop it finely.

7  Remove the skillet from the oven and let the chops rest, loosely covered with aluminum foil, for about 5 minutes. Arrange the chops on top of the cabbage on the platter, sprinkle with the remaining bacon, and drizzle any pan juices over the top. Serve immediately.

# SPICED PORK MEDALLIONS WITH APPLES, ONIONS, AND THYME

SERVES 4 ▪ PREP TIME: 10 MINUTES ▪ COOK TIME: 25 MINUTES

4 (6-ounce) boneless center-cut pork medallions

Kosher salt

Freshly ground black pepper

2 tablespoons extra-virgin olive oil

1 large onion, sliced

2 tablespoons apple cider vinegar

1 tablespoon unsalted butter

1 cooking apple, like Rome, Gravenstein, or Golden Delicious, peeled, halved, cored, and sliced

2 tablespoons thinly sliced fresh sage leaves

½ cup chicken broth

1 tablespoon whole-grain mustard

1 tablespoon minced fresh thyme leaves

*This is a beautiful dish to celebrate in-season apples in the fall, but you can enjoy it any time of year. Pork medallions are rounds of meat sliced from the lean pork tenderloin. Searing them in a hot skillet and finishing them in a hot oven ensures that they stay nice and moist and cook quickly. Smothering them with cooked apples and onions helps, too.*

1  Pat the pork medallions dry with paper towels, and season them generously with salt and pepper.

2  In a 12-inch cast iron skillet over medium-high heat, heat the olive oil. When the oil begins to shimmer, add the medallions to the pan and cook until nicely browned on the bottom, about 4 minutes. Turn the medallions over and cook until the second side is browned, about 3 more minutes. Transfer the pork to a plate, cover loosely with aluminum foil, and set aside.

3  With the skillet over medium heat, add the onion. Season with a pinch of salt and pepper and cook, stirring, until softened, about 6 minutes. Stir in the vinegar and cook, stirring and scraping up the browned bits from the bottom of the skillet with a spatula. Transfer the onions to the plate with the pork.

4 Increase the heat to medium-high, and add the butter to the skillet. When the butter melts, add the apple and sage and cook, stirring occasionally, until the apple begins to turn golden brown, about 3 minutes. Add the broth, mustard, and thyme and continue to cook until the apples are soft, about 2 minutes.

5 Return the cooked onions to the skillet, along with any juices that have accumulated on the plate, and cook until the liquid reduces a bit, about 2 minutes. Place the pork medallions on top of the onions and apples, nestling them down into the mixture. Heat until the pork is heated through, 3 to 5 minutes.

6 Place 1 pork medallion on each of 4 serving plates, pile a quarter of the apples and onions on top of each, and serve.

**SEASONAL SWAP:**
*In the summer, try substituting fresh figs or plums in place of the apples for a different take on this dish.*

# PAN-SEARED PORK CHOPS WITH FRESH HERBS, WILTED ARUGULA, AND RED WINE REDUCTION

SERVES 4 ▪ PREP TIME: 10 MINUTES ▪ COOK TIME: 20 MINUTES

2 tablespoons extra-virgin olive oil

3 tablespoons butter, divided

4 (1-inch-thick) bone-in rib pork chops (2½ to 3 pounds total)

Kosher salt

Freshly ground black pepper

4 garlic cloves, thinly sliced

1½ cups red wine

½ cup beef broth

2 fresh rosemary sprigs

4 fresh thyme sprigs

6 fresh sage leaves

1 tablespoon balsamic vinegar

5 ounces baby arugula

**QUICK & EASY**

*A trio of fresh herbs—rosemary, thyme, and sage—and a robust red wine reduction give this hearty dish a rustic appeal. The arugula is wilted by the hot chops and sauce when they are placed on top, making this a one-skillet meal.*

1 In a large cast iron skillet over high heat, heat the olive oil and 2 tablespoons of butter. Season the pork chops generously on both sides with salt and pepper. When the butter is melted and the oil and pan are very hot, add the chops and cook until golden brown on both sides, 2 to 3 minutes per side. Transfer the chops to a plate.

2 Lower the heat to medium-high and add the garlic. Cook, stirring frequently, until it turns golden, about 3 minutes. Add the wine and cook, stirring, until reduced by half, about 3 minutes more. Stir in the broth, rosemary, thyme, and sage. Return the chops to the pan and cook, shaking the pan now and then, for 5 minutes. Add the vinegar and cook 2 minutes more, until the chops are cooked through.

3 While the chops are cooking, arrange the arugula on a serving platter. Transfer the chops to the serving platter, arranging them on top of the arugula. Let the sauce continue to reduce if necessary until it is very thick. Add the remaining 1 tablespoon of butter and swirl until it is incorporated.

4 Season with additional salt and pepper if needed, then pour the sauce, along with the herbs and garlic, over the chops and arugula on the platter and serve.

# STIR-FRIED MANGO BEEF WITH BROCCOLI

SERVES 4 ■ PREP TIME: 10 MINUTES ■ COOK TIME: 15 MINUTES

½ cup chicken broth

3 tablespoons ketchup

3 tablespoons rice vinegar

3 tablespoons lower-sodium soy sauce

3 tablespoons sugar

1 tablespoon cornstarch

1½ teaspoons chili-garlic paste

12 ounces top sirloin or skirt steak, cut into strips

Kosher salt

Freshly ground black pepper

2 tablespoons peanut or vegetable oil

1 yellow onion, halved and thinly sliced

1 large head broccoli, florets separated, stalks peeled and thinly sliced

1 yellow or orange bell pepper, seeded and cut into strips

2-inch piece fresh ginger, peeled and minced

2 garlic cloves, minced

1 large (about 13 ounces) mango, peeled and diced

2 tablespoons chopped fresh cilantro

*This is a more exotic and refined version of the sweet and sour dishes you get in American Chinese restaurants. The mango is succulent and sweet, and its flavor pairs beautifully with the richness of the beef. A hint of spice adds a welcome counterpoint to the sweet fruit.*

1 In a large bowl, whisk together the broth, ketchup, vinegar, soy sauce, sugar, cornstarch, and chili-garlic paste.

2 Season the steak strips with salt and pepper and add them to the broth mixture in the bowl, tossing to coat well. Set aside.

3 In a 12-inch cast iron skillet over medium-high heat, heat the oil. When the oil begins to shimmer, add the onion and broccoli stalks and cook, stirring, for about 2 minutes. Add the broccoli florets, bell pepper, ginger, and garlic and cook, stirring, until the florets begin to soften, about 3 minutes.

4 Add the meat and its marinade to the pan and cook, stirring frequently, until the meat begins to brown, about 5 minutes. Stir in the mango and reduce the heat to medium. Cook for 3 minutes more.

5 Serve hot, garnished with the cilantro.

**PERFECT PAIRING:** *Serve this sweet-spicy dish with steamed rice and plenty of ice-cold beer.*

# PAN-SEARED RIB-EYE STEAKS WITH GORGONZOLA BUTTER AND GREEN BEANS

SERVES 4 ▪ PREP TIME: 5 MINUTES ▪ COOK TIME: 15 MINUTES

### FOR THE GORGONZOLA BUTTER

- ¼ cup crumbled Gorgonzola cheese, at room temperature
- 4 tablespoons butter, at room temperature

### FOR THE GREEN BEANS

- 2 tablespoons extra-virgin olive oil, divided
- 1 pound green beans, trimmed
- ½ cup water
- ½ teaspoon kosher salt, plus more for seasoning
- ¼ teaspoon freshly ground black pepper, plus more for seasoning

### FOR THE STEAK

- 4 rib-eye steaks, at room temperature
- 1 tablespoon chopped fresh parsley

*Cast iron pans and thick, juicy steaks are a match made in heaven. The high heat of the skillet is ideal for getting a good sear on the meat to seal in all the flavorful juices. Steam-sautéing the beans in the same skillet before cooking the steaks minimizes cleanup. And the rich, flavorful Gorgonzola butter is a truly decadent finishing touch.*

**To make the Gorgonzola butter**

In a small bowl, stir together the Gorgonzola and butter until well blended. Refrigerate until ready to serve.

**To cook the beans**

In a 12-inch cast iron skillet, heat 1 tablespoon of olive oil. Add the green beans and water. Cook the green beans until the water evaporates, about 4 minutes. Season the beans with ½ teaspoon of salt and ¼ teaspoon of pepper. Continue to cook, stirring, until the beans begin to brown and blister a bit, about 3 more minutes. Transfer the beans to a serving platter and wipe out the skillet.

**To cook the steak**

1 Season both sides of each steak generously with salt and pepper.

2 In the skillet over medium heat, heat the remaining 1 tablespoon of oil, swirling the pan to coat well. Place the steaks in the skillet and cook for 2 minutes on the first side. Turn them over and cook for 2 minutes on the second side. Cook longer if you prefer a more well-done steak. You may need to work in batches. If so, remove the first batch to a plate and tent loosely with aluminum foil while cooking the second batch, then move them to serving plates while resting the second batch (as described in the next step).

3 Remove the skillet from the heat and tent loosely with foil. Let the steaks rest in the skillet for 5 minutes.

4 Serve the steaks with the green beans, topping each steak with a spoonful of Gorgonzola butter and a sprinkling of parsley.

ESSENTIAL TECHNIQUE:
*Two of the best steak-cooking tips relate less to actually cooking the steak and more to how you treat the steak before and after cooking. First, take the steak out of the refrigerator 30 to 60 minutes before cooking, and let it come to room temperature to ensure that you can get a nice sear on the outside without overcooking the center. Second, let the steak rest for at least 5 minutes after cooking to allow the fibers to reabsorb the juices.*

# SEARED FLANK STEAK OVER ARUGULA-RADISH SALAD WITH BACON AND RAISIN-BALSAMIC DRESSING

SERVES 4 ▪ PREP TIME: 10 MINUTES ▪ COOK TIME: 15 MINUTES

1 pound flank steak

¾ teaspoon kosher salt

½ teaspoon freshly ground
black pepper

2 tablespoons extra-virgin
olive oil, divided

6 strips bacon, diced

1 small shallot, diced

1 tablespoon raisins

¼ cup balsamic vinegar

1 teaspoon sugar

1 teaspoon Dijon mustard

6 cups arugula
(1 [5-ounce] package)

5 radishes, halved
and thinly sliced

*This quick steak salad utilizes the high heat of the cast iron skillet to perfectly sear a flank steak, crisp up bacon, and make a flavorful balsamic dressing with the pan drippings. Raisins add a sweet note to balance out the salty bacon, arugula adds a kick of pepper, and radishes bring bright color and a crisp bite.*

1  Season the steak on both sides with the salt and pepper.

2  In a 12-inch cast iron skillet over medium-high heat, heat 1 tablespoon of olive oil. Add the steak and cook until nicely browned on both sides, about 3 minutes per side. Transfer the steak to a cutting board to rest while you prepare the rest of the dish.

3  In the skillet over medium-high heat, cook the bacon, stirring occasionally, until crisp, about 5 minutes. Transfer the bacon to a paper towel–lined plate to drain.

4  Reduce the heat to medium and add the shallot and raisins. Cook, stirring, just until the shallot is softened, about 3 minutes. Add the vinegar and sugar and cook, stirring, for 1 more minute. Remove the skillet from the heat.

5 Pour the vinegar mixture into a heat-safe bowl. Add the remaining 1 tablespoon of oil and the mustard, and whisk to combine.

6 In a large bowl, toss together the arugula, radishes, and about half of the dressing. Cut the steak into ¼-inch-thick slices.

7 Divide the salad mixture among 4 serving plates, top each with one-quarter of the sliced steak, sprinkle the bacon over the salads, and drizzle with the remaining dressing. Serve immediately.

# HEARTY BEEF AND BARLEY STEW

SERVES 4 ▪ PREP TIME: 10 MINUTES ▪ COOK TIME: 50 MINUTES

2 tablespoons vegetable oil

1 pound top sirloin,
   cut into 1-inch pieces

¼ cup chopped onion

1 garlic clove, minced

1 (14-ounce) can beef broth

1 (8-ounce) can tomato sauce

1 cup water

2 carrots, chopped

1 tomato, seeded and chopped

1 zucchini, chopped

1 cup medium pearl barley

2 teaspoons Italian seasoning

¼ teaspoon kosher salt

⅛ teaspoon freshly ground
   black pepper

*This is a classic weeknight dinner that's perfect for busy families. It's full of nutrition, uses common, budget-friendly ingredients, and everyone loves it. I like to make a batch of this and have leftovers throughout the week. It turns into a tasty soup with just a bit more beef broth added.*

1  In a 12-inch cast iron skillet over medium-high heat, heat the vegetable oil. Add the beef and onion and cook, stirring frequently, until the beef is browned, about 4 minutes. Stir in the garlic and cook for 1 minute more. Drain off the excess fat.

2  Stir in the broth, tomato sauce, and water and bring to a boil. Stir in the carrots, tomato, zucchini, barley, Italian seasoning, salt, and pepper and reduce the heat to low. Simmer, stirring occasionally, until the barley and beef are tender, about 45 minutes.

3  Serve warm.

ESSENTIAL TECHNIQUE: *When you have hours to let your stew simmer on the stove, you can use tougher, less expensive cuts of meat. But you can still make a delicious stew even if you're short on time by using a more tender, but still budget-friendly, cut of meat like top sirloin.*

# FRITTATA WITH BROCCOLI RABE, FONTINA, AND SAUSAGE

SERVES 6 ▪ PREP TIME: 10 MINUTES ▪ COOK TIME: 30 MINUTES

12 large eggs

½ cup whole milk

¾ cup grated Fontina cheese, divided

1 teaspoon kosher salt

½ teaspoon freshly ground black pepper

2 tablespoons vegetable oil

½ medium onion, chopped

½ pound fresh Spanish chorizo, diced, or hot Italian sausage links, casings removed

1 bunch broccoli rabe, coarsely chopped

*Frittatas are a super-easy one-skillet meal for a busy weeknight. This version includes spicy sausage, creamy Fontina cheese, and healthy broccoli rabe, but you can substitute any meat, cheese, or veggies you have in your refrigerator. Frittatas keep really well, so I love to prepare this for dinner one night and then eat leftovers for breakfasts or lunches throughout the week.*

1 Preheat the broiler.

2 In a medium bowl, whisk the eggs. Add the milk, ½ cup of cheese, and the salt and pepper, and whisk to combine. Set aside.

3 In a 12-inch cast iron skillet over medium heat, heat the vegetable oil. Add the onion and sausage and cook, stirring occasionally, until the sausage is browned and the onion is soft, about 7 minutes. Stir in the broccoli rabe and cook, stirring occasionally, until tender, about 8 minutes more.

4 Reduce the heat to low and add the egg mixture to the skillet. Cook, occasionally shaking the skillet, just until the edges are set, 10 to 12 minutes.

5 Sprinkle the remaining ¼ cup of cheese over the top and place the skillet under the broiler. Broil until the center of the frittata is set and the cheese is melted and golden brown, about 4 minutes.

6 Cut into wedges and serve warm.

# THE BEST BACON CHEESEBURGERS

SERVES 4 ▪ PREP TIME: 10 MINUTES ▪ COOK TIME: 25 MINUTES

4 slices (about 12 ounces) thick-cut bacon

1 medium red onion, thinly sliced

¼ cup mayonnaise

2 tablespoons extra-virgin olive oil, divided

1 tablespoon freshly squeezed lemon juice

Kosher salt

Freshly ground black pepper

¾ pound ground chuck

¾ pound ground sirloin

6 ounces Brie, sliced

4 brioche burger buns, split

*Fancy brioche buns, a lemony mayonnaise spread, creamy Brie, salty bacon, and sweet-savory caramelized onions make this a burger you won't soon forget. A cast iron skillet is the perfect vessel to make the whole meal happen, with just one pan to wash.*

1 In a 12-inch (or larger) cast iron skillet over medium-high heat, cook the bacon, about 4 minutes. Transfer to a paper towel–lined plate to drain. Split each strip in half.

2 Remove all but about 2 tablespoons of bacon fat from the skillet. Add the onion and cook over medium heat, stirring frequently, until it is very soft and golden brown, about 10 minutes. Transfer the onions to a bowl or plate.

3 While the onions are cooking, in a small bowl, whisk to combine the mayonnaise, olive oil, and lemon juice, and season with salt and pepper.

4 In a large bowl, mix the ground chuck and ground sirloin together, seasoning generously with salt and pepper. Divide the mixture into 4 equal portions and form each portion into a burger patty about ½ inch thick.

5 Heat the skillet over medium-high heat. Cook the burgers in the skillet until the bottom is nicely browned, about 5 minutes. Turn the burgers over, top with the Brie, and cook until the second side is browned, the cheese is beginning to melt, and the burgers are medium-rare, about 5 minutes more (for a more well-done burger, add a minute or 2 to the cooking time for each side).

6 On each of 4 plates, spread the cut sides of each bun with the mayonnaise mixture. Top the bottom half of each bun with a burger patty. Place 2 pieces of bacon on top of each burger and pile some of the onions on top of the bacon. Top with the burger bun tops and serve immediately.

**PERFECT PAIRING:**
*A crisp green salad with a tart vinaigrette would be the perfect way to round out this meal without weighing your guests down. Of course, no one would fault you if you chose to serve a side of crispy French fries or onion rings, too.*

# CHAPTER FOUR
# WEEKEND MEALS

On the weekends I like to be a little more leisurely in the kitchen. I try to save recipes with longer cooking times for a Saturday or Sunday when I'm not in a rush to get dinner on the table. The weekend is also a great time for recipes that require hands-free steps like waiting for meat to marinate or dough to rise. You'll find plenty of delicious weekend meals in this chapter, all of which still deliver on simplicity and ease, requiring just your cast iron skillet.

# VEGETARIAN

## WEEKEND MEALS

# PESTO PIZZAS WITH ZUCCHINI, EGGPLANT, AND GOAT CHEESE

SERVES 4 ▪ PREP TIME: 20 MINUTES, PLUS 2 HOURS TO RISE ▪ COOK TIME: 15 MINUTES

## FOR THE CRUST

1½ cups warm water

1 packet (2¼ teaspoons) active dry yeast

2 teaspoons sugar or honey

½ cup semolina flour

2¾ cups all-purpose flour

2 tablespoons extra-virgin olive oil

1 teaspoon kosher salt

## FOR THE PIZZAS

2 small zucchini, cut lengthwise into ¼-inch-thick slices

1 small eggplant, cut lengthwise into ¼-inch-thick slices

1 small red onion, halved and sliced

Kosher salt

Freshly ground black pepper

1 tablespoon extra-virgin olive oil

½ cup pesto (store-bought or homemade)

1 (5½-ounce) log soft fresh goat cheese

Chopped fresh basil leaves, for garnish

*With this recipe, you can make 2 medium pizzas using a 10- or 12-inch skillet, or you can make 4 individual-size pizzas using small (7-inch) skillets or 1 large pizza using a large (16- or 17-inch) skillet.*

**To make the crust**

1 In a large bowl (or the bowl of your stand mixer), sprinkle the yeast and sugar over the water, and stir to mix. Let sit for about 10 minutes, until the mixture becomes frothy.

2 Add the semolina and all-purpose flours, the olive oil, and the salt, and mix by hand or using the dough hook in a stand mixer for about 10 minutes. The dough should be smooth and springy.

3 Cover the bowl with a clean dishtowel and set it in a warm spot on your countertop to rise until it is doubled in size, 1½ to 2 hours.

4 If you are making smaller pizzas, divide the dough into 2 or more equal-size balls, depending on how many pizzas you plan to make. Cover the dough balls with the towel until you are ready to shape them.

**To make the pizzas**

1  In a medium bowl, season the zucchini, eggplant, and onion slices with salt and pepper, and toss with the olive oil.

2  Heat a cast iron skillet over medium-high heat. When hot, add the vegetables in a single layer (you'll need to cook them in batches or use more than one skillet) and cook until beginning to soften and turn golden on the bottom, about 2 minutes. Flip the vegetables over and cook until the second side is softened and golden, about 2 minutes more. Repeat with all of the vegetables.

3  Press or roll one of the dough balls into a circle roughly the size of your cast iron skillet. Spread some of the pesto onto the crust and top with some of the vegetables and goat cheese, dividing the toppings evenly among the pizzas.

4  Bake the pizza in the skillet in the preheated oven for 10 to 12 minutes, rotating it after 5 or 6 minutes, until the crust is golden brown and crisp.

5  Transfer the pizza to a cutting board, slice, and serve garnished with basil.

SEASONAL SWAP:
*One of the great things about pizza is that it is super versatile. If you don't have zucchini and eggplant, you can substitute other vegetables such as halved cherry tomatoes, chopped artichoke hearts, thinly sliced winter squash, or caramelized onions.*

# FARINATA WITH OVEN-ROASTED TOMATOES, ONIONS, AND GOAT CHEESE

SERVES 4 ▪ PREP TIME: 10 MINUTES
COOK TIME: 55 MINUTES ▪ TOTAL TIME: 1 HOUR, 15 MINUTES

¾ cup chickpea flour

1 cup water

3 tablespoons extra-virgin olive oil, divided

2 teaspoons chopped fresh rosemary leaves

½ teaspoon kosher salt, plus a pinch

¼ teaspoon freshly ground black pepper, plus a pinch

1 pint cherry tomatoes, halved

1 small onion, thinly sliced

⅛ teaspoon red pepper flakes

3 garlic cloves, minced

3 ounces fresh goat cheese

*Farinata is an Italian chickpea pancake (a similar dish is called socca in France) that is usually cooked in heavy copper pans in very hot wood-burning ovens. Here the cast iron skillet serves as a baking stone. The skillet itself gets very hot in the oven as the tomatoes and onions roast so that it crisps the bottom of the farinata similar to the way a pizza oven would.*

1 Preheat the oven to 450°F.

2 In a medium bowl, whisk to combine the chickpea flour with the water, 1 tablespoon of olive oil, the rosemary, ½ teaspoon of salt, and ¼ teaspoon of pepper. Set aside to rest for 30 minutes.

3 While the batter is resting, in a 10-inch cast iron skillet, combine the tomatoes, onion, red pepper flakes, garlic, 1 tablespoon of the remaining oil, and a pinch of salt and pepper, tossing to coat the vegetables with the oil. Spread the vegetables out in a single layer, transfer the skillet to the oven, and roast for 20 minutes, stirring once. Transfer the mixture to a bowl or plate and wipe out the skillet.

4 Increase the oven heat to 500°F (or as hot as your oven goes). Add the remaining 1 tablespoon of oil to the skillet, swirling to coat the bottom. Give the batter a stir and pour it into the skillet. Transfer to the oven and bake for 20 minutes.

5 Top the chickpea cake with the onion and tomato mixture and crumble the goat cheese over the top. Return the skillet to the oven and bake until the center of the chickpea cake is set, another 12 minutes.

6 Remove from the oven and let stand for 10 minutes before serving. Cut into wedges and serve.

**DID YOU KNOW?**
*Chickpea flour, also called besan or gram flour, is made of finely ground chickpeas (garbanzo beans) and is naturally gluten-free and high in protein and iron. It is used in many cuisines, from southern Europe and the Middle East to India and Burma, in soups, fritters, flatbreads, pasta, and sweets. You can find it in the international foods aisle in many supermarkets, in health food stores, or in Indian or Middle Eastern markets.*

# RADISH AND CHARD RISOTTO WITH PARMESAN

SERVES 4 ▪ PREP TIME: 10 MINUTES ▪ COOK TIME: 35 MINUTES

2 tablespoons butter

2 tablespoons extra-virgin olive oil

2 large shallots, finely chopped

1½ teaspoons fresh thyme leaves

2 garlic cloves, minced

8 to 10 Swiss chard leaves, ribs removed, leaves julienned

1 pound radishes, diced

1½ teaspoons kosher salt

1 cup short-grain Italian rice such as Arborio, carnaroli, or Vialone Nano

⅓ cup dry white wine

4 to 4½ cups vegetable broth, kept warm over low heat

½ cup freshly grated Parmesan cheese, plus more for garnish

¼ teaspoon freshly ground black pepper

2 tablespoons toasted pine nuts, for garnish

*Something magical happens when you cook radishes. These little beauties, usually seen raw in salads or as an afterthought garnish, turn tender and juicy and their flavor mellows. With still a hint of pepper, they take on an unexpected sweetness. Cooking them with risotto lends the entire dish a hint of pale pink color. Paired with the green chard, it makes a beautiful dish for a spring meal.*

1 In a 12-inch cast iron skillet over medium heat, heat the butter and olive oil. When the oil is hot and the butter melted, add the shallots. Cook, stirring occasionally, until the shallots are soft and golden, about 4 minutes.

2 Stir in the thyme and garlic and continue to cook, stirring, for 2 minutes more. Stir in the chard, radishes, and salt and cook until the chard wilts and the radishes just begin to brown, about 3 minutes more.

3 Add the rice and cook, stirring thoroughly so that all of the rice is coated with the oil.

4 Add the wine and cook, stirring, until it evaporates, 2 to 3 minutes. Add the broth, about ½ cup at a time, cooking and stirring continuously after each addition until the liquid is mostly absorbed before adding the next ½ cup of broth.

5 Continue adding broth in this manner until the rice is creamy and tender and most of the broth has been used (you may end up with ½ cup or so leftover). This will take about 20 minutes.

6 Stir in the cheese and pepper, and serve immediately, topped with the pine nuts and additional cheese.

**ESSENTIAL TECHNIQUE:**
*Risotto isn't as difficult to prepare as some make it out to be, and many have offered shortcuts to the process, but the fact remains that the best risotto requires close tending. Slowly adding warm broth and stirring continuously as the risotto cooks yields the creamiest risotto and helps prevent the dish from turning to unappetizing mush. It's a perfect dish for a leisurely weekend evening when you don't mind spending a bit of time at your stove.*

# SKILLET PIZZA WITH SHAVED ASPARAGUS AND GOAT CHEESE

SERVES 4 ▪ PREP TIME: 25 MINUTES, PLUS 10 MINUTES TO SIT AND 2 HOURS TO RISE
COOK TIME: 12 MINUTES

### FOR THE CRUST

1½ cups warm water

1 packet (2¼ teaspoons) active dry yeast

2 teaspoons sugar or honey

½ cup semolina flour

2¾ cups all-purpose flour

2 tablespoons extra-virgin olive oil

1 teaspoon kosher salt

### FOR THE PIZZAS

1 pound asparagus (medium thickness), trimmed and shaved lengthwise with a vegetable peeler into long ribbons

2 teaspoons extra-virgin olive oil

1 (5½-ounce) log soft fresh goat cheese

2 garlic cloves, minced

3 tablespoons chopped fresh marjoram

2 tablespoons chopped fresh flat-leaf parsley

Kosher salt

Freshly ground black pepper

¼ teaspoon red pepper flakes

Lemon, sliced into wedges, for garnish

*Whoever first thought of cooking pizza in a cast iron skillet was truly brilliant. The high, even heat of the skillet acts like a baking stone, giving the crust a divine texture that is the perfect balance between crispy and chewy. Topping it with an herbed goat cheese mixture and shaved asparagus makes it extra fancy.*

**To make the crust**

1 In a large bowl (or the bowl of your stand mixer), sprinkle the yeast and sugar over the warm water, and mix to combine. Let sit for about 10 minutes, until the mixture becomes frothy.

2 Add the semolina and all-purpose flours, the olive oil, and the salt, and mix by hand or using the dough hook in a stand mixer for about 10 minutes. The dough should be smooth and springy.

3 Cover the bowl with a clean dish towel and set it in a warm spot on your countertop to rise until doubled in size, 1½ to 2 hours.

4 Divide the dough into 2 equal-size balls and cover the dough balls with the towel until you are ready to shape them.

5 Press or roll one of the dough balls into a circle roughly the size of your cast iron skillet.

**To make the pizzas**

1 Preheat the oven to 500°F.

2 In a medium bowl, toss the asparagus ribbons with the olive oil.

3 In a small bowl, stir to combine the cheese, garlic, marjoram, and parsley, and season with salt and pepper.

4 Spread half of the cheese mixture all over the pizza crust, leaving a half-inch border around the edges. Scatter half of the asparagus ribbons on top of the cheese, and sprinkle half of the red pepper flakes over the top.

5 Transfer the skillet to the oven and bake until the crust is golden brown and crisp, 10 to 12 minutes, rotating it after 5 to 6 minutes.

6 Transfer the pizza to a cutting board, squeeze a bit of lemon juice over the top, slice, and serve. Repeat with the second ball of dough and the rest of the toppings.

ESSENTIAL TECHNIQUE:
*This recipe gives instructions for making 2 medium pizzas using a 10- or 12-inch skillet, but you can adjust the recipe to make several individual-size pizzas using small (7- or 8-inch) skillets or 1 large pizza using a large (16- or 17-inch) skillet.*

# VEGETARIAN SAMOSAS WITH FRESH HERB CHUTNEY

SERVES 4 ▪ PREP TIME: 20 MINUTES ▪ COOK TIME: 20 MINUTES

## FOR THE CHUTNEY

1 or 2 serrano peppers, coarsely chopped

1 (1-inch) piece peeled fresh ginger

1 cup fresh cilantro leaves

1 cup fresh mint leaves

½ cup chopped red onion

½ teaspoon kosher salt

¼ teaspoon sugar

¼ cup freshly squeezed lemon juice

1 tablespoon water

## FOR THE SAMOSAS

2½ cups mashed cooked and peeled baking potatoes

½ cup cooked yellow lentils

2 tablespoons minced fresh mint

2 teaspoons curry powder

2 teaspoons butter, at room temperature

½ teaspoon ground cumin

½ teaspoon kosher salt

1 cup fresh or frozen (thawed) petite green peas

20 egg roll wrappers

1 egg, lightly beaten

2 tablespoons vegetable oil, plus more as needed

*These spicy little bites make a great dish for a party or just a fun finger food dinner. Though they are quick and easy to make, filling and frying samosas might be a little daunting after a long day at work. On a leisurely weekend afternoon, though, this can be a fun family activity with a delicious outcome.*

**To make the chutney**

In a blender or food processor, process the peppers, ginger, cilantro, mint, onion, salt, sugar, lemon juice, and water until smooth.

**To make the samosas**

1  In a medium bowl, mix the potatoes, lentils, mint, curry powder, butter, cumin, and salt. Add the peas, stirring gently to incorporate.

2  Place 1 egg roll wrapper at a time on a cutting board, keeping the rest of the wrappers covered with a dish towel to keep them from drying out. Cut the wrapper into two equal-size long rectangles. Use a bit of the beaten egg to moisten the edges of the wrapper, and place about 1 tablespoon of the potato mixture on each rectangle, toward the bottom. Fold up from one corner of the rectangle over the filling toward the opposite edge of the wrapper to make a triangle. Continue to fold as you would a flag, so that you end up with a neatly packed triangle. Repeat the process until you have used up all of the wrappers and the filling.

3 In a 12-inch (or larger) cast iron skillet over medium-high heat, heat the vegetable oil, swirling to completely coat the bottom of the pan. When the oil begins to shimmer, add the samosas in a single layer and cook until golden brown on the bottom, about 1 minute. Turn over and cook until the second side is golden brown, about 1 minute more. Transfer to a paper towel–lined plate to drain, and repeat until all of the samosas are cooked.

4 Serve hot, with the chutney on the side for dipping.

**ESSENTIAL TECHNIQUE:**
*Use leftover cooked potatoes and lentils for this dish. If you don't happen to have those on hand, they're easy to make. For the potato, place a couple of baking potatoes in the microwave and cook on high for 5 to 10 minutes, until they are tender, then peel and mash them. For the lentils, put them in a saucepan on the stove, cover with water, bring to a boil, then simmer until they are tender, 15 to 20 minutes, and drain.*

# RATATOUILLE WITH GARLIC-HERB BREAD CRUMB TOPPING

SERVES 4 ▪ PREP TIME: 25 MINUTES ▪ COOK TIME: 1 HOUR, 10 MINUTES

## FOR THE SAUCE

4 large ripe tomatoes, cut into wedges (or substitute 1 [15-ounce] can diced tomatoes)

3 garlic cloves

1 red bell pepper, seeded

½ medium yellow onion

3 tablespoons extra-virgin olive oil

1 tablespoon freshly squeezed lemon juice

2 tablespoons fresh oregano leaves

1 teaspoon kosher salt

½ teaspoon freshly ground black pepper

½ to 1 teaspoon red pepper flakes

## FOR THE RATATOUILLE

3 small yellow squash, cut into ¼-inch-thick rounds

3 small zucchini, cut into ¼-inch-thick rounds

2 Asian eggplants, cut into ¼-inch-thick rounds

1 red bell pepper, seeded and cut into ¼-inch-wide by 2-inch-long strips

*Ratatouille is a classic French peasant dish that originated in the Provençal region of southern France. It is loaded with summer vegetables—tomatoes, eggplant, summer squash, and bell peppers—and cooked into a comforting stew. This version departs from the classic with a crisp bread crumb topping that's enriched with Parmesan cheese and studded with garlic and fresh herbs.*

Preheat the oven to 375°F.

**To make the sauce**

In a blender or food processor, process the tomatoes, garlic, bell pepper, onion, olive oil, lemon juice, oregano, salt, pepper, and red pepper flakes until smooth.

**To make the ratatouille**

1 In a 12-inch cast iron skillet, spread around three-quarters of the sauce to cover the bottom of the pan.

2 Beginning at the center of the skillet and working your way out, arrange the vegetable slices standing on their edges in an alternating pattern of yellow squash, then zucchini, then eggplant, then red bell pepper. Drizzle the remaining sauce over the top and cover with a piece of parchment paper cut to the size and shape of the skillet. Bake for 1 hour.

**To make the bread crumb topping**

1 While the vegetables are baking, in a small bowl, stir together the bread crumbs, cheese, parsley, oregano, and garlic. Stir in the melted butter.

2 Increase the oven heat to 450°F. Remove the skillet from the oven, discard the parchment paper, and sprinkle the bread crumb mixture over the top, spreading it evenly. Return the skillet to the oven and cook until the topping is browned and crisp, about 10 minutes more.

3 Serve immediately.

FOR THE BREAD
CRUMB TOPPING

1 cup panko bread crumbs

½ cup freshly grated
Parmesan cheese

1 tablespoon minced flat-leaf
parsley

1 tablespoon minced fresh
oregano

1 garlic clove, minced

2 tablespoons melted butter

**ESSENTIAL
TECHNIQUE:**
*To save time and keep
your veggie slices uni-
form in thickness, you
can slice them in a food
processor fitted with a
slicing blade, or use a
handheld mandolin.*

# ROASTED WINTER SQUASH AND WHITE BEAN CASSOULET

SERVES 8 ▪ PREP TIME: 20 MINUTES ▪ COOK TIME: 1 HOUR, 40 MINUTES

2 tablespoons plus
    ½ teaspoon extra-virgin
    olive oil, divided

4 garlic cloves, sliced

1 large onion, sliced

4½ cups (½-inch) peeled and
    cubed butternut squash
    (about 2 pounds)

1½ teaspoons minced
    fresh thyme leaves

½ teaspoon kosher salt

¼ teaspoon freshly ground
    black pepper

4 (16-ounce) cans cannellini
    or other white beans,
    rinsed and drained

1 dried bay leaf

½ cup vegetable broth

2 (1-ounce) slices white bread

2 tablespoons grated fresh
    Parmesan cheese

1 tablespoon chopped fresh
    flat-leaf parsley

*This vegetarian version of the classic French dish* cassoulet *replaces the meat with roasted butternut squash. Caramelized onions and garlic add depth of flavor, and a crisp, garlicky bread crumb topping finishes it off.*

1  Preheat the oven to 375°F.

2  In a 12-inch cast iron skillet over medium-high heat, heat 2 tablespoons of olive oil. Add the garlic and onion and cook, stirring frequently, until the onion is softened, about 5 minutes. Reduce the heat to medium-low and continue to cook, stirring occasionally, until the onion is very soft and golden brown, about 20 minutes. Remove from the heat.

3  Add the squash, thyme, salt, pepper, beans, and bay leaf to the skillet and stir to combine. Stir in the broth and spread the vegetables out into an even layer.

4  Cover the vegetables in the skillet with a piece of parchment paper cut to the size and shape of the skillet. Transfer the skillet to the oven and bake until the squash is tender, about 1 hour.

5  Meanwhile, in a food processor or blender, pulse the bread into coarse crumbs. In a small bowl, mix the bread crumbs together with the Parmesan and the remaining ½ teaspoon of oil.

6  Remove the skillet from the oven, discard the parchment paper, and sprinkle the bread crumb mixture evenly over the vegetable mixture. Return the skillet to the oven and bake until the topping is crisp and browned, about another 15 minutes.

7  Serve immediately, garnished with the parsley.

# FISH & SEAFOOD

## WEEKEND MEALS

# SEAFOOD PAELLA ON THE GRILL

SERVES 4 TO 6 ▪ PREP TIME: 15 MINUTES ▪ COOK TIME: 45 MINUTES

2 tablespoons extra-virgin olive oil, divided

½ small sweet onion, chopped

2 garlic cloves, minced

4 ounces Spanish chorizo, sliced (optional)

4 ripe tomatoes, chopped or 1 (15-ounce) can whole peeled San Marzano tomatoes

1 (8-ounce) jar roasted red peppers, sliced

¼ cup white wine

2 cups Arborio rice

1 teaspoon kosher salt, plus more for seasoning

Freshly ground black pepper

4 cups chicken broth

1 teaspoon ground smoked paprika

Pinch saffron

⅓ pound peeled and deveined shrimp

⅓ pound cleaned squid, bodies cut into rings

⅓ pound bay scallops

8 live mussels in their shells, scrubbed and rinsed

Juice of 2 lemons

Chopped fresh flat-leaf parsley, for garnish

*Seafood paella cooked on the grill is a great dish for a backyard party on a warm summer evening. Glasses of chilled cava (the Spanish version of Champagne) would add to the festive tone and pair beautifully with the flavorful seafood.*

1 Preheat your grill to high heat and place a 12-inch cast iron skillet on the grill to preheat.

2 Add 1 tablespoon of olive oil and the onion and garlic to the hot skillet and cook, stirring frequently, until the onion is softened, about 5 minutes. Add the chorizo (if using) and continue to cook, stirring occasionally, until the sausage is browned, about 3 minutes more. Stir in the tomatoes and red peppers and cook for another 5 minutes.

3 Deglaze the pan with the wine, stirring to scrape up any browned bits from the bottom, then stir in the rice, salt, and pepper. Cook, stirring, until the rice is well coated, about 3 minutes, then stir in the broth. Add the paprika and saffron and stir to mix. Cover the skillet with a lid, if you have one that fits, or a sheet of aluminum foil (be sure to use protected hands to fit the foil on top). Close the lid of the grill and cook for 20 minutes.

4 While the rice is cooking, in a medium bowl, toss the shrimp, squid, and scallops with the remaining 1 tablespoon of olive oil, and season with salt and pepper.

5 Lift the lid of the grill and carefully lift off the skillet lid. Scatter the shrimp, squid, and scallops over the rice, and add the mussels. Replace the skillet lid and close the grill lid. Cook until the seafood is cooked through and the rice is tender, about 10 minutes more.

6 Squeeze the lemon juice over the top and serve immediately, garnished with parsley.

**ESSENTIAL TECHNIQUE:** *You could make this on the stove top, as well, but the grill adds a smoky flavor to the dish.*

# CREOLE SHRIMP AND CHEDDAR GRITS

SERVES 4 ▪ PREP TIME: 10 MINUTES ▪ COOK TIME: 40 MINUTES

2 tablespoons butter

1 onion, finely chopped

2 garlic cloves, minced

1 teaspoon kosher salt

3½ cups water

½ cup heavy cream

1 cup grits (not instant)

1½ cups (about 6 ounces)
  shredded extra-sharp white
  Cheddar cheese, divided

3 eggs, lightly beaten

4 scallions, thinly sliced

½ teaspoon ground
  cayenne pepper

¼ teaspoon freshly ground
  black pepper

1½ pounds peeled and
  deveined large shrimp

*Shrimp and grits is a classic creole dish. It's not hard to make, but it usually uses multiple pots and pans. This version is cooked all in one skillet. First the grits are cooked with water and cream, then the whole dish is baked in the oven. The result is a creamy texture and rich flavor punctuated by the sharp cheese and a hit of cayenne.*

1 Preheat the oven to 450°F.

2 In a 12-inch cast iron skillet over medium heat, melt the butter. When the butter is melted and bubbly, add the onion and cook, stirring frequently, until softened, about 8 minutes. Add the garlic and cook, stirring, for 1 minute more. Stir in the salt.

3 Add the water and cream to the skillet and bring to a boil. Whisking constantly, whisk the grits into the liquid in a steady stream. Reduce the heat to low and cook, stirring often, until the grits are creamy, about 15 minutes. Turn off the heat.

4 In a medium bowl, whisk 1 cup of cheese together with the eggs, scallions, cayenne, and black pepper. Add the egg mixture to the grits and stir to mix well.

5 Arrange the shrimp on the grits and push them down so they are completely submerged. Sprinkle the remaining ½ cup of cheese over the top, and transfer the skillet to the oven. Bake until the cheese is melted and browned and the grits are hot, about 15 minutes.

6 Remove from the oven and let stand for a few minutes before serving.

# SALMON AND ASPARAGUS EN CROUTE WITH LEMON-HERB CRÈME FRAÎCHE

SERVES 4 ▪ PREP TIME: 10 MINUTES ▪ COOK TIME: 20 MINUTES

2 garlic cloves, grated

¼ cup crème fraîche

2 teaspoons finely grated
    lemon zest

1 teaspoon chopped
    fresh rosemary leaves

2 sheets (1 box) frozen puff
    pastry, thawed but very cold

1 boneless, skinless salmon
    fillet (about 1½ pounds)

Kosher salt

Freshly ground black pepper

1 pound asparagus,
    trimmed and peeled

1 egg, lightly beaten

*This is the best kind of one-skillet dinner—the kind that comes wrapped in a buttery, flaky puff pastry crust. This dish is easy to make since it uses store-bought puff pastry, but it is guaranteed to impress anyone you serve it to. Defrost the pastry in the refrigerator overnight.*

1 Preheat the oven to 450°F.

2 In a small bowl, stir together the garlic, crème fraîche, lemon zest, and rosemary.

3 Lay 1 sheet of puff pastry in a 12-inch (or larger) cast iron skillet. Lay the salmon fillet on top of the pastry, centering it. Season the salmon with salt and pepper. Spread the crème fraîche mixture over the top of the fillet, and lay the asparagus spears on top, lined up like pencils.

4 Place the remaining pastry sheet on top of the salmon. Press and crimp the edges to seal the two sheets of pastry together. Trim off any excess around the edges, leaving a border of about 1 inch. Use the tines of a fork to press a decorative pattern into the edges of the pastry. With a sharp knife, cut 3 slits of about 1 inch each in the top of the pastry so that steam can escape as the fish cooks. Brush the beaten egg over the pastry.

5 Transfer the skillet to the oven and bake until the pastry is puffed and golden brown, about 20 minutes.

6 Remove the skillet from the oven and let stand for 5 minutes before cutting into the pastry. Cut into slices and serve immediately.

# SALMON CONFIT WITH CRISP VEGETABLE SALAD

SERVES 4 ▪ PREP TIME: 10 MINUTES, PLUS 1 HOUR AND 35 MINUTES TO MARINATE AND REST
COOK TIME: 15 MINUTES ▪ TOTAL TIME: 2 HOURS

### FOR THE SALMON

4 (6-ounce) salmon fillets

2 cups extra-virgin olive oil, plus more for brushing

3 dried bay leaves

2 strips lemon rind

3 fresh thyme sprigs

1 teaspoon black peppercorns

½ teaspoon kosher salt, plus more for seasoning

2 cups vegetable oil

### FOR THE SALAD

2 fennel bulbs, thinly sliced

1 tablespoon snipped fresh chives

1 tablespoon chopped fresh dill

2 tablespoons freshly squeezed lemon juice

2 tablespoons extra-virgin olive oil

Freshly ground black pepper

*To confit something means to cook it slowly, submerged completely in fat. Cooking salmon this way keeps it moist and retains all of its rich flavor. It may seem like a lot of oil, but it won't absorb into the fish. The crisp fennel and tart lemon cut the richness of the fish with their freshness and acidity.*

**To make the salmon**

1 Place the salmon fillets skin-side down in a baking dish and brush all over with some olive oil. Scatter the bay leaves, lemon rind, thyme, peppercorns, and salt over the fish, cover, and refrigerate for 30 to 60 minutes. Remove the fish from the refrigerator about 20 minutes before cooking to let it come to room temperature.

2 Preheat the oven to 250°F.

3 In a 12-inch cast iron skillet over medium heat, heat the vegetable oil and olive oil until warm (about 150°F on an instant-read thermometer). Slip the salmon into the warm oil and transfer the skillet to the oven. Bake for 12 minutes. The salmon should be medium-rare. Add a few more minutes if you prefer it more well done. Remove the salmon from the oven and let it rest in the oil for about 15 minutes.

**To assemble the salad**

1  While the fish is resting, make the salad. In a medium bowl, toss together the fennel, chives, dill, lemon juice, and olive oil. Season with salt and pepper.

2  Carefully remove the fish from the oil and transfer it to a paper towel–lined plate to drain. Carefully remove the skin from each fillet.

3  Divide the vegetables among 4 serving plates. Top each salad mound with a salmon fillet, and serve immediately.

ESSENTIAL TECHNIQUE:
*You can use either wild or farmed salmon for this dish, but wild is a healthier and more sustainable choice. Because wild salmon is much leaner than farmed, it will cook faster and dry out more quickly. If using wild salmon, begin checking the fish for doneness once it has been in the oven for 8 minutes.*

# STUFFED CALAMARI BRAISED IN TOMATO SAUCE

SERVES 4 ▪ PREP TIME: 20 MINUTES ▪ COOK TIME: 1 HOUR

¼ cup plus 2 tablespoons extra-virgin olive oil, divided

12 calamari, cleaned, bodies left whole and tentacles chopped

1 cup dried bread crumbs

1 cup finely grated pecorino romano cheese

3 tablespoons finely chopped fresh flat-leaf parsley

2 tablespoons finely chopped fresh oregano

Kosher salt

Freshly ground black pepper

½ small onion, finely chopped

2 garlic cloves, finely chopped

¼ teaspoon dried oregano

2 teaspoons tomato paste

4 tablespoons red wine, divided

1 (28-ounce) can whole peeled tomatoes with their juice

1 dried bay leaf

2 teaspoons balsamic vinegar

*Because it uses squid, a slightly unusual ingredient, and each squid body is stuffed with a flavorful bread crumb mixture, this dish has an air of sophistication. But squid is actually quite easy to work with, and it's budget friendly, too. The squid becomes deliciously tender when braised in a rich tomato sauce. You can buy the squid already cleaned, but make sure you get both the bodies and the tentacles.*

1 In a 12-inch cast iron skillet over medium heat, heat ¼ cup of olive oil. When the oil is hot, add the chopped calamari tentacles and cook, stirring, for 1 minute. Remove the skillet from the heat and transfer the tentacles and oil to a medium bowl. Add the bread crumbs, pecorino romano, parsley, and oregano and season with salt and pepper, stirring to combine.

2 In the skillet over medium-high heat, heat the remaining 2 tablespoons of oil. Add the onion, garlic, and oregano and cook, stirring frequently, until the onion is softened, about 5 minutes. Stir in the tomato paste and cook, stirring, until it begins to brown, about 2 minutes. Add 3 tablespoons of wine, the tomatoes with their juice (crushing the tomatoes with your hands as you add them), and the bay leaf.

3 Reduce the heat to medium-low and simmer until the sauce has thickened, about 20 minutes. Stir in the remaining 1 tablespoon of wine and the vinegar. Season with salt and pepper and remove from the heat.

4 Preheat the oven to 350°F.

5 Fill each calamari cavity about half full with the bread crumb mixture. Secure the opening closed with wooden toothpicks, if necessary. Place each filled calamari in the sauce in the skillet. When all the calamari are in the skillet, spoon sauce over so that they are covered.

6 Transfer the skillet to the oven and bake until the squid are cooked and the filling is hot, about 30 minutes.

7 Serve immediately.

# POULTRY

## WEEKEND MEALS

# CHICKEN AND SAUSAGE CASSOULET

SERVES 4 ▪ PREP TIME: 10 MINUTES ▪ COOK TIME: 30 MINUTES

4 boneless, skinless
   chicken thighs

Kosher salt

Freshly ground black pepper

4 tablespoons extra-virgin
   olive oil, divided

4 pork sausages
   (about ¾ pound),
   pricked

1 medium onion, thinly sliced

4 garlic cloves, minced,
   divided

1 (28-ounce) can whole
   peeled tomatoes

1 (15-ounce) can cannellini
   beans, rinsed and drained

1 cup chicken broth

1½ cups fresh or store-bought
   bread crumbs

1 medium shallot, thinly sliced

1 tablespoon minced
   fresh rosemary leaves

*Traditional cassoulet can take hours, even days, to make. Make this quick version instead by browning two types of meat in a very hot skillet on the stove top, then simmering it with vegetables, canned beans, and broth. Finally, add a garlic-and-herb bread crumb topping, brown it under the broiler, and voilà! Classic French comfort food in 40 minutes!*

1 Preheat the broiler.

2 Season the chicken thighs generously with salt and pepper.

3 In a 12-inch cast iron skillet over medium-high heat, heat 2 tablespoons of olive oil. Add the sausages and chicken thighs and cook until browned, about 4 minutes. Turn the sausages and chicken over and cook until the second side is browned, about 4 minutes more. Add the onion to the pan and cook, stirring frequently, until the onion is softened, about 3 minutes. Add 2 of the minced garlic cloves and cook, stirring, for another 30 seconds.

4 Add the tomatoes, beans, and broth, season with salt and pepper, and bring to a simmer. Cook, stirring occasionally and breaking up the tomatoes with a spoon or spatula, until the liquid has thickened, about 15 minutes. Spread into an even layer.

5 Meanwhile, in a small bowl, stir together the bread crumbs and the remaining 2 minced garlic cloves with the shallot, rosemary, and the remaining 2 tablespoons of olive oil.

6 Top the chicken mixture with the bread crumb mixture. Place the skillet under the broiler and cook until crisp and golden brown on top, about 2 minutes.

7 Serve immediately.

# CHICKEN POT PIE WITH BUTTERNUT SQUASH AND GREENS

SERVES 4 TO 6 ▪ PREP TIME: 20 MINUTES

COOK TIME: 1 HOUR, 10 MINUTES ▪ TOTAL TIME: 1 HOUR, 40 MINUTES

4 tablespoons butter

1 small onion, finely diced

4 garlic cloves, minced

1 tablespoon chopped fresh sage leaves

1 small bunch kale, ribs removed, leaves julienned

Kosher salt

Freshly ground black pepper

¼ cup all-purpose flour

2 cups chicken broth

1 cup whole milk

1½ cups ½-inch-dice butternut squash (about ½ small squash)

1 pound boneless, skinless chicken breast, cut into ½-inch cubes

1 sheet frozen puff pastry, thawed overnight in the refrigerator

1 egg, lightly beaten

*Chicken pot pie may be the ultimate Sunday dinner comfort food. This version is full of nutritious vegetables and white chicken meat bathed in a rich gravy and topped with a flaky, buttery puff pastry crust. You could substitute a store-bought or homemade pie crust for the puff pastry if you like.*

1 Preheat the oven to 425°F.

2 In a 10-inch skillet over medium-high heat, melt the butter. Add the onion and cook, stirring frequently, until softened, about 5 minutes. Reduce the heat to medium-low and stir in the garlic and sage. Continue to cook, stirring occasionally, for 2 minutes more. Stir in the kale, season with salt and pepper, and cook, stirring frequently, until the kale is wilted, about 4 minutes. Sprinkle the flour over the mixture in the skillet and cook, stirring constantly, for 4 minutes more.

3 Slowly add the broth and milk, whisking to combine well, then stir in the squash. Bring to a simmer, reduce the heat to medium-low, and simmer, stirring occasionally, until the squash is tender and the liquid has thickened, about 15 minutes. Stir in the chicken, and season with salt and pepper. Remove the skillet from the heat.

4 Unfold the sheet of pastry and place it over the skillet, tucking the edges into the skillet. Brush the egg over the pastry and then, with a sharp knife, cut 4 slits, each about 1 inch long, into the top of the pastry to allow steam to escape during cooking.

5 Transfer the skillet to the oven and bake until the crust just begins to brown, about 20 minutes. Reduce the temperature to 375°F and continue to bake until the crust is crisp and golden brown all over, another 15 to 20 minutes.

6 Remove the skillet from the oven and let stand for 10 minutes before serving. Serve hot.

**ESSENTIAL TECHNIQUE:**
*The pie can be made ahead of time and refrigerated for up to 24 hours. Bring it to room temperature and then reheat it in a 375°F oven before serving.*

# CHICKEN STEW WITH HERBED DUMPLINGS

SERVES 4 TO 6 ■ PREP TIME: 20 MINUTES ■ COOK TIME: 1 HOUR

## FOR THE STEW

1 pound boneless, skinless chicken breasts

2 tablespoons extra-virgin olive oil

2 medium carrots, finely diced

2 celery stalks, finely diced

1 large onion, finely diced

1 tablespoon chopped fresh thyme leaves

1 teaspoon kosher salt

½ teaspoon freshly ground black pepper

4 tablespoons butter

¼ cup all-purpose flour

2 tablespoons whole milk

6 cups chicken broth

1 cup fresh or frozen peas

## FOR THE DUMPLINGS

2 cups all-purpose flour

2 teaspoons baking powder

¾ teaspoon kosher salt

1 cup whole milk

2 tablespoons butter, melted

2 tablespoons minced fresh chives

2 tablespoons chopped fresh parsley

*Here is another quintessential Sunday comfort food dish, this one with a decidedly Southern bent. To shorten time spent on this recipe without any loss of flavor, use leftover roast chicken or even a rotisserie chicken from the market. Making the dumplings from scratch, though, is what really elevates this dish to special weekend meal status. They are light and fluffy and infused with the flavor of fresh herbs.*

**To make the stew**

1  In a 12-inch cast iron skillet over medium-high heat, cover the chicken breasts with water. Bring to a boil and then simmer for about 15 minutes, reducing the heat as needed to keep the water at a gentle simmer, until the chicken is cooked through.

2  Transfer the chicken breasts to a plate to cool. When the chicken is cool enough to handle, chop it into ½-inch dice. Pour out the cooking water and wipe out the skillet.

3  Preheat the oven to 350°F.

4  In the skillet over medium-high heat, heat the olive oil. Add the carrots, celery, and onion and cook, stirring, until the onion is translucent and the vegetables begin to soften, about 5 minutes. Stir in the thyme, salt, and pepper and cook, stirring, for 1 more minute.

5  Add the butter to the skillet, and when it has melted, sprinkle the flour over it, stirring to mix well. Cook until the butter and flour begin to brown, about 5 minutes. Stir in the milk and broth and bring the mixture to a boil. Reduce the heat to medium, add the peas, and cook at a simmer for about 10 minutes.

**To make the dumplings and bake**

1 Meanwhile, in a medium bowl, whisk together the flour, baking powder, and salt. Stir in the milk, butter, and chives just until incorporated.

2 Stir the chicken into the stew, then drop the dumpling batter onto the top of the stew by the rounded spoonful.

3 Transfer the skillet to the preheated oven and bake for 15 minutes. Place a piece of aluminum foil over the skillet (use oven mitts to protect your hands!) and continue to bake for another 10 minutes.

4 Serve immediately.

# OVEN-ROASTED CHICKEN WITH PARSNIPS AND FENNEL

SERVES 4 TO 6 ▪ PREP TIME: 10 MINUTES
COOK TIME: 55 MINUTES ▪ TOTAL TIME: 1 HOUR, 15 MINUTES

1 whole chicken
(3½ to 4 pounds)

Kosher salt

Freshly ground black pepper

3 tablespoons extra-virgin
olive oil, divided

1 fennel bulb, cut lengthwise
into ½-inch-thick slices

2 large parsnips, peeled,
cut into ½-inch-thick slices
on the diagonal

6 to 8 scallions

3 wide strips lemon zest
(using a vegetable peeler)

*There's just something about roasting a whole bird that always makes the meal seem like a Big Deal. Whenever I do it, I am surprised by how easy it is, and how special the result. A freshly roasted chicken on a bed of seasonal vegetables is the kind of home-cooked meal dreams are made of.*

1 Preheat the oven to 425°F.

2 On a plate, generously season the chicken inside and out with salt and pepper.

3 In a 12-inch cast iron skillet over medium-high heat, heat 1 tablespoon of olive oil. When the oil begins to shimmer, add the chicken to the skillet, breast-side down. Cook until it turns golden brown on the bottom, then carefully rotate the chicken to brown it on all sides. This step will take about 15 minutes total. Transfer the browned chicken to a clean plate.

4 Add the remaining 2 tablespoons of oil to the skillet along with the fennel, parsnips, scallions, and lemon zest. Season with salt and pepper, then place the browned chicken, breast-side up, on top of the vegetables.

5 Transfer the skillet to the oven and roast until the chicken is cooked through (it should register at least 165°F on an instant-read thermometer, or release clear juices when you cut into the thigh meat at the thigh joint), 35 to 40 minutes.

6 Transfer the chicken to a carving board and let it rest for a minimum of 10 minutes before carving.

7 Serve the chicken and vegetables with the pan drippings spooned over the top.

**SEASONAL SWAP:** *You can use any root vegetables you have available for this dish with excellent results. Baby potatoes, sweet potatoes, turnips, rutabaga, carrots, and onions would all be perfect in this dish.*

# CRISPY DUCK BREAST WITH PEPPERS AND ONIONS

SERVES 4 ▪ PREP TIME: 10 MINUTES, PLUS AT LEAST 2 HOURS TO MARINATE
COOK TIME: 20 MINUTES

2 or 3 duck breasts
(about 2 pounds total)

3 garlic cloves, minced

4 tablespoons melted butter

1 tablespoon brown sugar

3 tablespoons extra-virgin
olive oil, divided

3 tablespoons
Worcestershire sauce

1 teaspoon hot pepper sauce
(such as Tabasco or Crystal)

½ teaspoon kosher salt

1 teaspoon freshly ground
black pepper

1 red onion, cut into
thin wedges

1 red bell pepper,
seeded and cut into strips

1 yellow bell pepper,
seeded and cut into strips

1 orange bell pepper,
seeded and cut into strips

2 tablespoons snipped
fresh chives

*A simple marinade adds deep flavor to the duck breasts before they are seared to crisp-on-the-outside, pink-in-the-middle perfection. The peppers and onions are sautéed in the rendered duck fat, making them especially delectable.*

1 Score the fatty side of the duck breasts in a crosshatch pattern, cutting through the skin and fat layer but not into the meat.

2 In a large bowl, whisk together the garlic, butter, brown sugar, and 2 tablespoons of olive oil with the Worcestershire sauce, hot pepper sauce, salt, and pepper. Add the duck breasts, onion, and peppers and toss to coat. Marinate, covered, in the refrigerator, for at least 2 hours.

3 Preheat the oven to 400°F.

4 Remove the duck, onions, and peppers from the marinade (discard the marinade). Pat the duck breasts dry with paper towels.

5 In a large cast iron skillet over medium-high heat, heat the remaining 1 tablespoon of oil. Add the duck breasts, skin-side down, and cook until the skin is a deep golden brown and crispy and the fat begins to render, about 5 minutes. Turn the breasts over and sear for 4 to 5 minutes on the second side, until golden brown.

6  Transfer the skillet to the preheated oven and cook for 5 minutes more for medium-rare. Remove from the oven and transfer the duck breasts to a cutting board. Let rest for at least 5 minutes.

7  While the duck is resting, remove all but about 2 tablespoons of fat from the skillet, and set it over medium-high heat. Add the onions and peppers and cook, stirring frequently, until they soften and begin to char in spots, about 5 minutes.

8  Slice the duck into ½-inch-thick slices and return it to the skillet with the peppers and onions. Sprinkle the chives over the top and serve immediately.

# PORK, BEEF, & LAMB

## WEEKNIGHT MEALS

# CITRUS-MARINATED STEAK TACOS

SERVES 4 ▪ PREP TIME: 10 MINUTES, PLUS AT LEAST 6 HOURS TO MARINATE
COOK TIME: 15 MINUTES

**FOR THE STEAK**

Juice of 2 limes

Juice of 1 lemon

Juice of 1 orange

¼ cup red wine

2 garlic cloves, minced

1 tablespoon dried oregano

1 teaspoon kosher salt

1 teaspoon freshly ground
   black pepper

1 pound flank or skirt steak

**FOR THE TACOS**

8 corn tortillas

2 cups shredded lettuce

4 radishes, sliced

1 cup salsa

Lime wedges, for garnish

**PERFECT PAIRING:**
*This meal begs for ice-cold Mexican beers or tart margaritas. If you want to make this meal into a party spread, add chips, guacamole, and a pot of pinto or refried beans.*

*I'm sure I've said this before, but I believe there is no better way to cook a steak than in a cast iron skillet. This one is marinated in a tangy blend of citrus juices and savory herbs. The cooked steak is sliced thinly and used as a taco filling. If you're feeling ambitious, make the Handmade Corn Tortillas on page 154.*

**To make the steak**

1 In a large, resealable plastic bag, combine the lime juice, lemon juice, orange juice, wine, garlic, oregano, salt, and pepper. Add the steak and turn or shake to coat. Refrigerate for at least 6 hours and as long as 24 hours.

2 Heat a large cast iron skillet (large enough to fit the steak) over high heat. Remove the steak from the marinade (discard the marinade), and pat dry with paper towels. Add the steak to the hot skillet and cook until browned, 5 to 7 minutes. Turn the steak over and cook for 5 to 7 minutes more.

3 Transfer the steak to a cutting board, tent loosely with aluminum foil, and rest for 5 minutes before slicing into ¼-inch-thick slices.

**To make the tacos**

1 While the steak rests, wipe out the skillet and heat the tortillas for 1 to 2 minutes on each side.

2 Place 2 tortillas on each of 4 serving plates. Top each with several strips of steak and an equal portion of the lettuce, radishes, and salsa. Garnish with a lime wedge and serve immediately.

# PORT-MARINATED ROAST PORK WITH APPLES

SERVES 4 ▪ PREP TIME: 15 MINUTES, PLUS AT LEAST 4 HOURS TO MARINATE
COOK TIME: 55 MINUTES

1 (2-pound) boneless center-cut pork loin, trimmed

Kosher salt

Freshly ground black pepper

1 cup ruby port

¼ cup brown sugar

2 garlic cloves, minced

1 tablespoon fresh thyme leaves

3 tablespoons extra-virgin olive oil, divided

4 tablespoons cold butter, divided

2 medium shallots, thinly sliced

2 apples, such as Cortland or Rome, peeled, cored, and cut into 8 slices

2 tablespoons balsamic vinegar

1 cup apple cider

*This is an impressive dinner party dish, but it is deceptively simple to make. Flavored with port, shallots, thyme, and apples, it's a great fall or winter dish, and it's elegant enough to deserve a place on your holiday table. You can substitute a robust red wine, like a Zinfandel, for the port if you like.*

1 Season the roast generously with salt and pepper. In a large bowl, whisk together the port, brown sugar, garlic, thyme, and 1 tablespoon of olive oil. Add the pork roast and turn to coat. Cover and refrigerate for at least 4 hours or overnight.

2 Preheat the oven to 400°F.

3 Remove the pork from the marinade (reserving the marinade) and pat it dry. In a 12-inch (or larger) cast iron skillet over high heat, heat the remaining 2 tablespoons of oil. Add the pork to the pan and cook, turning occasionally, until it is golden brown on all sides, about 3 minutes per side. Transfer the meat to a plate.

4 Add 2 tablespoons of butter and the shallots to the skillet. Cook, stirring frequently, until the shallots are softened, about 6 minutes. Add the apples, stir to combine, then move the apples and shallots around the outer edge of the pan, making an empty space in the center. Place the roast in the center, pouring in any juices that have collected on the plate.

5  Transfer the skillet to the oven and roast until the meat registers 145°F on an instant-read thermometer inserted into the center, 30 to 35 minutes.

6  Remove the skillet from the oven and transfer the roast to a cutting board. Tent the roast loosely with aluminum foil. Transfer the apples and shallots to a serving platter.

7  Return the skillet to high heat and add the vinegar. Cook, scraping up any browned bits from the bottom of the skillet, for about 2 minutes, then add the apple cider and the reserved marinade. Cook, stirring frequently, until reduced by half, about 6 minutes. Turn off the heat and whisk in the remaining 2 tablespoons of butter. Season with salt and pepper if needed.

8  Slice the roast into ½-inch-thick pieces, and arrange them over the apple and shallot mixture on the platter. Drizzle some of the sauce over the top. Place the remaining sauce in a pitcher or bowl to pass at the table, and serve.

# CAJUN-SPICED STUFFED PORK CHOPS

SERVES 4 ▪ PREP TIME: 15 MINUTES ▪ COOK TIME: 45 MINUTES

3 teaspoons extra-virgin olive oil, divided

8 ounces smoked tasso ham or andouille sausage

½ yellow onion, finely diced

½ bell pepper, seeded and finely diced

4 garlic cloves, finely chopped

4 scallions, chopped

⅓ cup chopped fresh flat-leaf parsley

1 tablespoon hot pepper sauce (such as Tabasco or Crystal)

1 teaspoon kosher salt

1 teaspoon ground paprika

½ teaspoon garlic powder

½ teaspoon freshly ground black pepper

¼ teaspoon ground cayenne pepper

1 teaspoon dried oregano

1 teaspoon dried thyme

4 thick-cut pork chops

*Stuffed with vegetables, herbs, and smoky ham or spicy sausage and then rubbed with a mix of Cajun seasonings, these pork chops make a fine centerpiece for a Sunday dinner. If you're using the andouille sausage, you might want to use less of the hot pepper sauce—unless you like a serious kick!*

1 Preheat the oven to 350°F.

2 In a 12-inch (or larger) cast iron skillet over medium-high heat, heat 1 teaspoon of olive oil. Add the ham, onion, bell pepper, and garlic. Cook, stirring frequently, until the onion is softened and beginning to turn golden, about 6 minutes. Turn off the heat and stir in the scallions, parsley, and hot pepper sauce.

3 In a small bowl, stir together the salt, paprika, garlic powder, black pepper, cayenne, oregano, and thyme.

4 With a sharp knife, cut a slit like a pocket into each pork chop. Try to make the opening as small as possible while creating the pocket as large as possible on the inside of the pork chop (see tip).

5 Stuff the meat and vegetable filling into the pockets of the chops using a spoon, and secure the openings with toothpicks. Season the outside of the chops with the spice mixture.

6 In the same skillet, heat the remaining 2 teaspoons of olive oil over medium-high heat. Add the chops and brown them on both sides, about 3 minutes per side.

7 Transfer the skillet to the oven and bake until the pork chops register 155°F using an instant-read thermometer, about 30 minutes.

8 Remove the skillet from the oven and let the chops rest for at least 5 minutes before serving.

ESSENTIAL TECHNIQUE:
*To cut the pocket in a pork chop, lay the chop on a cutting board. Place your non-dominant hand flat on top of the chop to hold it down. With the other hand, use the tip of a sharp knife, held parallel to the cutting board, to cut into the chop, cutting a pocket that goes almost, but not quite, all the way through.*

# BEEF CHILI TAMALE PIE

SERVES 6 ▪ PREP TIME: 10 MINUTES
COOK TIME: 45 MINUTES ▪ TOTAL TIME: 1 HOUR, 10 MINUTES

## FOR THE FILLING

6 tablespoons unsalted butter

1 pound ground chuck

1 medium onion, finely diced

4 garlic cloves, thinly sliced

2 tablespoons ancho
chili powder

¼ teaspoon ground cayenne
pepper (optional)

1 tablespoon ground cumin

1 teaspoon ground coriander

1 cup fresh or frozen (thawed)
corn kernels

1 (15-ounce) can black beans,
drained and rinsed

1 (28-ounce) can whole peeled
tomatoes, drained and
crushed by hand

1 cup chicken broth

1 cup (about 4 ounces) grated
sharp Cheddar cheese

3 scallions, thinly sliced

½ cup minced fresh cilantro
(leaves and fine stems)

Kosher salt

Freshly ground black pepper

*This is a delightfully updated version of the ho-hum dump-and-bake dish I remember from childhood. The chili is made by browning aromatics and meat and layering in spices. The topping, a light, buttery cornbread layer that soaks up all the delicious chili flavors, is also made from scratch. It's a guaranteed family favorite.*

**To make the filling**

1 Preheat the oven to 425°F.

2 In a 12-inch cast iron skillet over medium heat, melt the butter. After it melts, keep cooking it, shaking the pan now and then, until the butter just begins to brown, 3 to 5 minutes. Transfer to a heatproof bowl and set aside.

3 Increase the heat to high. Add the meat and cook, stirring frequently and breaking up any clumps with a spatula, until the meat is browned, about 8 minutes. Stir in the onion and garlic and continue to cook, stirring, until the onion is softened, about 4 minutes. Stir in the chili powder, cayenne (if using), cumin, and coriander and cook, stirring, for 30 seconds.

4 Stir in the corn, beans, tomatoes, and broth and bring to a simmer. Reduce the heat to low, stir in the cheese, and cook, stirring occasionally, until the mixture becomes thick, about 5 minutes.

5 Turn off the heat. Add the scallions and cilantro and season with salt and pepper. Spread the mixture out into an even layer.

**To make the cornbread topping and assemble**

1 In a large bowl, mix together the cornmeal, flour, sugar, salt, baking powder, and baking soda. In a medium bowl, whisk together the eggs, sour cream, and buttermilk. Slowly add the melted butter to the egg mixture, stirring constantly. Stir the wet ingredients into the flour mixture until well incorporated.

2 Drop the cornbread batter on top of the beef mixture by the heaping spoonful, then spread it out into an even layer with a spatula or the back of a spoon.

3 Transfer the skillet to the oven and bake until the cornbread is golden brown and a tester inserted into the center comes out clean, about 20 minutes.

4 Let cool for about 15 minutes before serving. Serve hot.

FOR THE CORNBREAD TOPPING

1 cup finely ground
    yellow cornmeal

1 cup all-purpose flour

¼ cup sugar

1 teaspoon kosher salt

2 teaspoons baking powder

¼ teaspoon baking soda

2 eggs

¾ cup sour cream

¼ cup buttermilk

# CLASSIC WINE-BRAISED BEEF STEW WITH VEGETABLES

SERVES 4 ▪ PREP TIME: 20 MINUTES ▪ COOK TIME: 2 HOURS

4 slices thick-cut bacon, diced

1½ pounds flatiron steak, top sirloin or chuck, trimmed and cut into 1-inch pieces

Pinch kosher salt, plus more for seasoning

Pinch freshly ground black pepper, plus more for seasoning

½ cup all-purpose flour

1 onion, finely diced

2 garlic cloves, minced

2 medium carrots, finely diced

2 celery stalks, finely diced

12 ounces cremini or button mushrooms, sliced

1 tablespoon tomato paste

2 cups dry red wine

1 cup chicken or beef broth

2 dried bay leaves

1 fresh thyme sprig

Chopped fresh flat-leaf parsley, for garnish

*A classic beef stew is about building layers of flavor. The bacon provides a base of salty, meaty, smoky flavor and all the fat needed to sear the beef and vegetables. Tomato paste, wine, garlic, onions, celery, carrots, mushrooms, and herbs add additional layers. Stew is one of those dishes that only get better with time, so you can make it a day ahead and reheat it before serving.*

1 In a 12-inch (or larger) cast iron skillet over medium-high heat, cook the bacon until crisp and golden, about 5 minutes. Remove the pan from the heat and transfer the bacon to a paper towel–lined plate. Drain all but about 2 tablespoons of fat from the pan.

2 Season the meat generously with salt and pepper, and dredge the pieces in the flour. Cook the meat in a single layer (you may need to sear the meat in batches to avoid crowding the pan) over medium-high heat. Cook the meat, turning occasionally, until it is browned on all sides, about 10 minutes total. Transfer the meat to a plate.

3 Add the onion, garlic, carrots, and celery to the skillet and continue to cook, stirring occasionally, over medium heat until the onion is softened, about 5 minutes. Add the mushrooms and cook, stirring, until they soften, about 5 minutes. Stir in the tomato paste and cook, stirring, for 1 minute more.

4 Deglaze the pan with the wine, using a wooden spoon or spatula to stir and scrape up the browned bits that have stuck to the bottom of the skillet. Add the broth, bay leaves, thyme, and a pinch of salt and pepper, and bring to a boil.

5 Cover the skillet with aluminum foil (carefully, with oven mitts on both hands), or an ovenproof lid if you have one, and transfer the skillet to the oven. Cook until the meat is fork tender, 1 to 1½ hours. Stir the bacon into the stew.

6 Serve hot, garnished with parsley.

**PERFECT PAIRING:**
*Serve this stew spooned over creamy mashed potatoes if you like. A robust red wine, like a Cabernet Sauvignon, Syrah, or Zinfandel, would complement the stew nicely.*

# SPAGHETTI BOLOGNESE

SERVES 4 ▪ PREP TIME: 10 MINUTES ▪ COOK TIME: 1 HOUR, 25 MINUTES

2 tablespoons extra-virgin olive oil

2 tablespoons butter

4 ounces pancetta or bacon, finely diced

2 onions, finely diced

2 carrots, finely diced

2 celery stalks, finely diced

2 garlic cloves, minced

1 teaspoon kosher salt

1 pound lean ground beef

1 cup milk

1 cup red wine

1 (28-ounce) can diced tomatoes with their juice

¼ cup tomato paste

2 teaspoons dried oregano

½ teaspoon red pepper flakes

12 ounces dried spaghetti, noodles broken in half, rinsed under cold water, and drained

½ to 1 cup water (if needed)

Freshly grated Parmesan cheese, for serving

*To make a good Bolognese sauce, you have to layer the ingredients and allow them to simmer together to develop deep, rich flavor. This version requires a number of steps and then simmers for a good long while, making it a great dish to prepare on a lazy Sunday afternoon. The pasta cooks right in the sauce, though, so you'll still only have one pan to wash.*

1 In a 12-inch cast iron skillet over medium-high heat, heat the olive oil and butter. Add the pancetta and onions and cook, stirring frequently, until the onions are soft and translucent, about 5 minutes. Add the carrots, celery, garlic, and salt and cook, stirring frequently, until softened, about 5 minutes.

2 Add the ground beef and cook, stirring and breaking up the meat with a spatula, until browned, 6 to 8 minutes. Stir in the milk and let simmer for about 5 minutes, until the liquid has mostly evaporated.

3 Stir in the wine and cook, stirring occasionally, until most of the liquid has evaporated, about 3 minutes.

4 Add the tomatoes with their juice, tomato paste, oregano, and red pepper flakes and stir to combine. Bring to a simmer and cook over medium-low heat, stirring occasionally, until the tomatoes break down and the sauce thickens, 30 to 45 minutes.

5 Add the pasta and push it under the liquid so that it is completely covered. If there isn't enough liquid, add water, and simmer until the pasta is tender and the sauce has thickened some more, about 15 minutes.

6 Serve hot, topped with Parmesan cheese.

# SPICED LAMB BURGERS WITH FETA AND HERBED YOGURT SAUCE

SERVES 4 ▪ PREP TIME: 15 MINUTES ▪ COOK TIME: 15 MINUTES

### FOR THE YOGURT SAUCE

1 cup plain Greek-style yogurt

1 garlic clove, minced

3 tablespoons chopped fresh chives

3 tablespoons finely chopped fresh flat-leaf parsley

2 teaspoons freshly squeezed lemon juice

Kosher salt

Freshly ground black pepper

### FOR THE BURGERS

1½ pounds ground lamb

¾ cup (about 4 ounces) crumbled feta cheese

1 small red onion, finely chopped

1 garlic clove, minced

3 tablespoons finely chopped fresh mint

3 tablespoons finely chopped fresh flat-leaf parsley

1 teaspoon ground cumin

1 teaspoon kosher salt

1 teaspoon freshly ground black pepper

Extra-virgin olive oil, for brushing

4 burger buns, split

4 romaine lettuce leaves

4 thin tomato slices

*With ground lamb, Greek seasonings, and tangy feta cheese, these burgers are really something special. Cooking them in cast iron gives them a golden-brown sear that seals in all of their delicious juices.*

**To make the yogurt sauce**

In a small bowl, whisk together the yogurt, garlic, chives, parsley, and lemon juice. Season with salt and pepper.

**To make the burgers**

1  In a medium bowl, combine the lamb, feta, onion, garlic, mint, parsley, cumin, salt, and pepper. Mix gently with your hands until well combined. Shape the mixture into 4 patties, each about ½ inch thick. Brush the patties lightly on both sides with olive oil.

2  Heat a 12-inch (or larger) cast iron skillet over medium-high heat. Cook the burgers in the skillet until nicely browned and cooked to desired doneness, about 5 to 7 minutes per side.

3  Put an open burger bun on each of 4 plates, set the burgers on the bottom halves of the buns, and top each with a spoonful of the herbed yogurt sauce, a lettuce leaf, and a tomato slice. Top with the top halves of the buns and serve immediately, offering the remaining yogurt sauce on the side.

**ESSENTIAL TECHNIQUE:** *When cooking burgers, it's tempting to press down on the patties, but do your best to resist the urge in order to keep all those delicious juices in your burger.*

# CHAPTER FIVE

# BREADS & ROLLS

# HANDMADE CORN TORTILLAS

MAKES ABOUT 14 TORTILLAS ▪ PREP TIME: 10 MINUTES ▪ COOK TIME: 15 MINUTES

2 cups masa harina,
   plus more if needed

½ teaspoon kosher salt

1½ cups hot water,
   plus more if needed

*Homemade corn tortillas may sound outrageously ambitious, but you'll be shocked by how easy they are to make. In fact, if you're like me, you'll wonder why you haven't been making them yourself. A tortilla press speeds up the process a bit, but it isn't a necessity. Masa harina is finely ground cornmeal. It can be found in the international foods aisle of many supermarkets, in Mexican markets, or online.*

1 In a medium bowl, stir together the masa harina and salt. Add the water and stir to mix well. Knead the dough with your hands for 1 minute. The dough will be very soft, light, and a bit springy. If it is too dry and crumbles, add more water 1 tablespoon at a time. If it feels too wet to form into balls, add more masa harina 1 tablespoon at a time.

2 Pinch off golf ball–size chunks of the dough and roll them in your hands to form balls, setting each ball aside and covering with a towel as you finish. Repeat until you have used up all the dough. You should have around 14 balls.

3 Lay a piece of plastic wrap out on your work surface, and place a ball on top. Top with another piece of plastic wrap. Pat or roll each ball out into a thin, 6-inch circle using either your hands or a rolling pin. If you are using a tortilla press, place plastic wrap on the bottom, top with a dough ball and a second piece of plastic, press, then remove the tortilla.

4 Continue until all of the balls have been flattened, keeping the flattened tortillas in a stack under a towel, or cook the tortillas one at a time as you flatten them.

5 To cook the tortillas, heat a 12-inch (or larger) cast iron skillet (or griddle if you have one) over medium-high heat. When the surface is very hot, add 2 tortillas without overlapping them.

6 Cook until the tortillas begin to puff a bit in spots and the sides begin to curl a bit, 1 to 2 minutes per side. When cooked, both sides should be dry and browned in spots. Wrap the cooked tortillas in a towel to keep them warm while you cook the rest.

7 Serve immediately or cool to room temperature and refrigerate (see tip) for up to 3 days. Reheat the tortillas in a hot skillet.

**ESSENTIAL TECHNIQUE:**

*These tortillas are best if cooked just before serving, but you can make the dough, form the balls, and flatten the tortillas up to a day ahead if you like. Keep the raw tortillas in the refrigerator, stacked with squares of parchment in between and wrapped in plastic wrap.*

# ONION NAAN

MAKES 10 NAAN ▪ PREP TIME: 20 MINUTES, PLUS 1 HOUR AND 20 MINUTES TO RISE
COOK TIME: 40 MINUTES

¾ cup whole milk

1 packet (2¼ teaspoons)
   active dry yeast

1 teaspoon sugar

3½ cups all-purpose flour,
   plus more for dusting

1 teaspoon kosher salt,
   plus more for sprinkling

1 small onion, finely chopped

1 cup plain, whole-milk yogurt
   (not Greek)

2 tablespoons melted ghee
   (clarified butter)
   or vegetable oil,
   plus more for greasing

*A clay oven–baked Indian flat bread, naan is a fantastic accompaniment to sop up flavorful Indian curries and other saucy dishes. It also makes a great crust for personal-size pizzas. Like any yeasted bread, preparation takes a while, but the small rounds of dough cook quickly in a hot skillet. Here the sustained high heat of the skillet acts like a baking stone, making your regular oven more like the traditional clay oven.*

1  In a small saucepan, over medium-low heat, heat the milk until it is hot to the touch, about 100°F. Transfer the hot milk to a small bowl, sprinkle the yeast and sugar over the top, and stir to mix. Let stand until the mixture becomes frothy, about 10 minutes.

2  In a large bowl, combine the flour and 1 teaspoon of salt. Stir in the yeast mixture, onion, yogurt, and 2 tablespoons of ghee. Mix to blend the ingredients well. The dough will be fairly wet and shaggy.

3  Lightly flour your work surface, and turn the dough out onto it. Knead with your hands until the dough becomes smooth (it will still be sticky), about 5 minutes.

4  Lightly oil a large bowl with ghee. Form the dough into a ball and place it in the bowl, turning to coat all over with the oil. Cover the bowl and place it in a warm spot on your countertop to rise until doubled in size, about 1 hour.

5 Punch the dough down and split it into 10 equal pieces. Dust your hands with flour and then roll each dough piece into a ball. Leave the balls on your work surface, cover with plastic wrap, and let rise for a second time, about 10 minutes.

6 Lightly coat a 12-inch (or larger) cast iron skillet with ghee, and heat over medium-high heat. Use your hands or a rolling pin to flatten each dough ball into a rough oval, about ⅛ inch thick. Sprinkle salt over the top and cook in the hot skillet until it puffs up and begins to blister in spots, about 2 minutes on each side.

7 Wrap the cooked naan in aluminum foil to keep warm while you cook the remaining pieces.

8 Serve warm.

**ESSENTIAL TECHNIQUE:**

*The dough can be made, risen, and shaped up to 4 hours ahead. Wrap in plastic wrap and refrigerate until about 20 minutes before you are ready to cook.*

# ROSEMARY FOCACCIA WITH SEA SALT

SERVES 6 TO 8 ▪ PREP TIME: 15 MINUTES, PLUS AT LEAST 10 HOURS TO RISE
COOK TIME: 25 MINUTES

3 ¼ cups bread flour or all-purpose flour

1 tablespoon kosher salt

½ teaspoon instant yeast

1 ¼ cups plus 3 tablespoons water

4 tablespoons extra-virgin olive oil, divided

2 tablespoons fresh rosemary leaves, very roughly chopped

Coarse sea salt

*This olive oil–enriched, herbed Italian flatbread is easy to make, requiring surprisingly little hands-on time, but it needs time to rise. It's a no-knead bread, meaning all you do is mix the ingredients and let the dough rise for a while (8 to 24 hours). Drenched in flavorful olive oil and sprinkled with fresh rosemary and flaky sea salt, it's delicious all on its own, but it's also great for sopping up sauces or making fancy sandwiches.*

1  In a large bowl, mix together the flour, salt, yeast, and water. Stir with a wooden spoon or your hands until the flour and water are fully incorporated. Cover the bowl with plastic wrap and let rise in a warm spot on your countertop for a minimum of 8 hours and as long as 24 hours, until the dough expands to fill the bowl.

2  Lightly flour your work surface, and turn the dough out onto it. Form it into a tight ball.

3  Add 2 tablespoons of olive oil to a 12-inch cast iron skillet. Place the ball in the pan and turn it so that it is thoroughly coated in oil. Place the ball seam-side down and press it with the palm of your hand to flatten it. Cover the skillet with plastic wrap and set aside to rise at room temperature for 2 more hours.

4 Preheat the oven to 550°F.

5 By now, the dough will have risen to almost fill the skillet. Use your fingers to press the dough out to the edges of the pan, popping any air bubbles you see. Drizzle the remaining 2 tablespoons of oil over the top, and sprinkle with the rosemary and sea salt.

6 Transfer the skillet to the oven and bake until the top and bottom are golden brown and the bottom is crisp when lifted from the skillet, 16 to 24 minutes.

7 Remove the skillet from the oven and transfer the bread to a cutting board. Let cool for a few minutes before slicing to serve.

**SEASONAL SWAP:** *This recipe is easily varied by adding different toppings. Top it with sliced ripe pears or figs in the fall, thinly sliced winter squash in the winter, shaved fennel in spring, or halved or whole cherry tomatoes or sliced red bell peppers in the summer. Olives, pine nuts, or Parmesan cheese would be lovely additions any time of year.*

# CHEDDAR-JALAPEÑO SKILLET CORNBREAD WITH FRESH CORN AND SCALLIONS

SERVES 8 ▪ PREP TIME: 10 MINUTES
COOK TIME: 30 MINUTES ▪ TOTAL TIME: 50 MINUTES

2½ tablespoons melted butter, plus more for preparing the skillet

1¼ cups stone-ground cornmeal

1 cup fresh corn kernels (from about 2 ears)

¾ teaspoon kosher salt

½ teaspoon baking soda

1 cup buttermilk

1 cup (about 4 ounces) shredded sharp Cheddar cheese

1 to 2 jalapeño peppers, seeded and minced

2 scallions, thinly sliced

1½ tablespoons honey

2 eggs, lightly beaten

**SEASONAL SWAP:**
*This cornbread is fantastic with plump kernels of sun-ripened summer corn fresh from the cob, but if good, fresh corn isn't available due to the season, feel free to substitute frozen (thawed) corn kernels.*

*Cooking cornbread in sizzling butter in a hot cast iron skillet creates a crispy outer edge that's so irresistible, I'm pretty sure you'll never cook cornbread in a regular cake pan again. If you prefer a milder version, substitute mild green chiles for the jalapeño. For extra authenticity, use bacon drippings to oil the pan instead of butter.*

1 Preheat the oven to 375°F.

2 Brush a 10-inch cast iron skillet with melted butter, and heat in the oven for 5 minutes.

3 In a large bowl, whisk together the cornmeal, corn, salt, and baking soda.

4 In a small bowl, stir together the buttermilk, cheese, jalapeños, scallions, 2½ tablespoons of melted butter, honey, and eggs. Whisk the wet ingredients into the dry ingredients until just combined.

5 Spoon the batter into the preheated skillet and bake until a tester inserted into the center comes out clean, about 30 minutes.

6 Remove the skillet from the oven and set on a wire rack. Allow the cornbread to cool in the skillet for 10 minutes before slicing into wedges. Serve warm or at room temperature.

# FLAKY BUTTERMILK BISCUITS

MAKES 12 BISCUITS ▪ PREP TIME: 15 MINUTES ▪ COOK TIME: 35 MINUTES

5 tablespoons melted butter, divided, plus ½ cup (1 stick) cold, unsalted butter

3 cups all-purpose flour

2 tablespoons baking powder

1 teaspoon fine sea salt

¼ cup sugar

1 cup buttermilk

¾ cup heavy cream

**ESSENTIAL TECHNIQUE:**

*Grating the butter is a Southern grandma's secret to flaky biscuits. Make sure the butter is very cold (freeze it first if possible), and use the large holes of a box grater to grate it. This makes the job of combining the butter and flour easy and also keeps the butter cold, which is key.*

*Who can resist flaky, buttery buttermilk biscuits? Whether you spread them with butter and jam or drench them in sausage gravy, they will make any meal seem extra special. Cooking them in a cast iron skillet will ensure that they have the flaky, crisp outer shell that makes them so addictive.*

1 Preheat the oven to 350°F.

2 In a 12-inch cast iron skillet, swirl 2 tablespoons of melted butter, coating the entire bottom and the sides of the pan.

3 In a large bowl, whisk together the flour, baking powder, salt, and sugar. Using the large holes of a box grater, grate the ½ cup of cold butter into the flour. Use a fork to mix the butter into the flour until it resembles a coarse meal. Stir in the buttermilk and cream. Continue to mix, either with a wooden spoon or your hands, until the dough comes together in a ball.

4 Lightly flour your work surface, and roll the dough out until it is about ¾ inch thick. Use a round biscuit or cookie cutter to cut out rounds, and place them in the buttered skillet.

5 Bake until golden brown, 30 to 35 minutes.

6 Remove from the oven and brush with the remaining 3 tablespoons of melted butter. Serve warm.

# PERFECT PARKER HOUSE ROLLS

MAKES ABOUT 12 ROLLS

PREP TIME: 20 MINUTES, PLUS 90 MINUTES TO RISE ▪ COOK TIME: 20 MINUTES

1½ cups milk

½ cup (1 stick) unsalted butter, cut into small pieces, plus 4 tablespoons melted

¼ cup sugar

1 packet (2¼ teaspoons) active dry yeast

½ cup warm water (about 110°F)

3 large eggs, lightly beaten

1½ teaspoons fine sea salt

6 to 8 cups all-purpose flour, divided, plus more for dusting

Vegetable oil, for greasing

1 tablespoon minced fresh rosemary leaves (optional)

Flaky sea salt (optional)

*Parker House rolls are a quintessentially American food, invented at Boston's Parker House Hotel in the late nineteenth century. They are tender, delicate, lightly sweetened, milk-based dinner rolls with a slightly crisp outer shell. Brushed with butter both before and after baking, they are perfectly addictive. I like them sprinkled with flaky sea salt and a bit of fresh rosemary, but leave these off and they make delightful breakfast rolls spread with (more) butter and jam.*

1  In a microwave-safe bowl or glass measuring cup, heat the milk for about 45 seconds in the microwave. Add the butter pieces and sugar, and stir until the butter is melted and the sugar is dissolved.

2  In a large mixing bowl or in the bowl of a stand mixer, combine the yeast, warm water, the milk mixture, eggs, salt, and 3 cups of flour. Mix with an electric mixer or dough hook until combined, 2 to 3 minutes.

3  Add the remaining 3 to 5 cups of flour in ½-cup increments until the dough comes together in a smooth ball. The dough should be soft and loose, but not sticky.

4  Transfer the dough to a lightly floured board and knead it for several minutes, adding more flour if needed to keep it from sticking, until it is very smooth, about 5 minutes. Shape the dough into a ball and place it in a lightly oiled bowl. Cover and let rise in a warm spot on your countertop until doubled in size, about 1 hour.

5 Lightly coat a 12-inch cast iron skillet with vegetable oil.

6 Transfer the risen dough to a lightly floured board and pat it out into a rough oval or rectangle. Divide the dough into 12 equal-size pieces and form them into balls. As the balls are formed, place them into the prepared skillet, leaving a bit of space between them.

7 Cover again and let rise on the countertop until they have expanded to fill the space in between the rolls, about 30 minutes more.

8 Meanwhile, preheat the oven to 350°F.

9 Brush the rolls with some melted butter and sprinkle with rosemary (if using). Transfer the skillet to the oven and bake until the rolls are golden brown on top, about 20 minutes.

10 Brush with a bit more melted butter, sprinkle with flaky sea salt (if using), and serve warm.

ESSENTIAL TECHNIQUE: *To make ahead, prepare the rolls through step 7, wrap them in plastic wrap, and store them in the refrigerator (for up to 24 hours) or freezer (for up to a month). Bring refrigerated rolls to room temperature by setting on the countertop for 30 to 60 minutes before brushing with butter and baking. For frozen rolls, defrost on the countertop for 2 to 3 hours.*

# CHEDDAR-SCALLION SKILLET SCONES

SERVES 8 ▪ PREP TIME: 10 MINUTES ▪ COOK TIME: 20 MINUTES

6 tablespoons very cold butter, cut into small pieces, plus more at room temperature for greasing

2 cups all-purpose flour, plus more for dusting

½ teaspoon fine sea salt

1 tablespoon baking powder

1 cup grated sharp Cheddar cheese

3 scallions, thinly sliced

2 large eggs

⅓ cup heavy cream

1 teaspoon hot pepper sauce (such as Tabasco or Crystal)

*These savory scones, laced with sharp Cheddar cheese and studded with scallions, are every bit as delicious as their sweeter counterparts. Serve these alongside scrambled eggs for breakfast or brunch, or enjoy them as a savory snack any time of day.*

1 Preheat the oven to 400°F, and grease a 10-inch cast iron skillet with room-temperature butter.

2 In a large bowl, whisk together the flour, salt, and baking powder. Work in the cold butter with your fingers to make a crumbly mixture. Mix in the cheese and scallions.

3 In a small bowl, whisk together the eggs, cream, and hot pepper sauce. Add the egg mixture to the dry ingredients and stir with a wooden spoon just until the mixture is uniformly moist.

4 Flour your hands and work surface and then knead the dough a few times. Form it into a ball, place it in the prepared skillet, and pat the dough out with your hands until it covers the bottom of the skillet and is about ¾-inch thick.

5 Transfer the skillet to the oven and bake until the top is nicely browned, 18 to 20 minutes.

6 Remove from the oven and let cool for several minutes before slicing into wedges to serve.

**ESSENTIAL TECHNIQUE:** *Using very cold butter is essential here. The bits of butter distributed throughout the dough melt in the oven, creating steam, which creates little air pockets. Place the butter in the freezer for 30 minutes and use a box grater to grate it.*

# IRISH SODA BREAD WITH RAISINS

MAKES 1 LARGE LOAF ▪ PREP TIME: 10 MINUTES ▪ COOK TIME: 40 MINUTES

4 tablespoons cold butter, cut into small pieces, plus more at room temperature for greasing

4 cups flour

2 tablespoons sugar

1 teaspoon fine sea salt

1 teaspoon baking soda

1 cup raisins

1 egg, lightly beaten

1½ to 2 cups buttermilk

*Soda bread, so called because it's leavened with baking soda instead of yeast, is easy to make. There are as many variations as there are Irish grandmothers. Traditionally, raisins and sugar would only have been added as a special treat, and they are what make this version so irresistible.*

1 Preheat the oven to 425°F, and lightly butter a 12-inch cast iron skillet.

2 Sift the flour, sugar, salt, and baking soda into a large bowl. Add the butter pieces and work them into the flour mixture with your hands until the mixture resembles a coarse meal. Mix in the raisins.

3 Stir the egg and 1½ cups of buttermilk into the flour mixture with a wooden spoon, mixing until the dough is very thick. Use your hands to knead the dough into a rough ball. Mix in more buttermilk 1 tablespoon at a time if the dough is too thick to knead. Place the dough in the prepared skillet and shape it into a round loaf. Score an "x" into the top of the dough, using a serrated knife.

4 Transfer the skillet to the preheated oven and bake for about 40 minutes.

5 When it's done, the top will be golden brown and the bottom will make a hollow sound when tapped with a knife. Place the bread on a wire rack and let cool for a few minutes before slicing. Serve warm or at room temperature.

# SAVORY ASIAGO, GARLIC, AND HERB MONKEY BREAD

SERVES 6 ▪ PREP TIME: 25 MINUTES, PLUS AT LEAST 1 HOUR, 45 MINUTES TO RISE
COOK TIME: 40 MINUTES

½ cup (1 stick) plus
2 tablespoons unsalted
butter, melted

1 cup milk, warm

⅓ cup water, warm

2 tablespoons sugar

1 tablespoon instant yeast

3¼ cups all-purpose flour,
plus more as needed

2 teaspoons fine sea salt

1 tablespoon extra-virgin
olive oil

2½ cups grated Asiago
cheese, divided

½ cup freshly grated
Parmesan cheese, divided

4 garlic cloves, minced

2 tablespoons chopped
fresh basil

2 tablespoons chopped
fresh oregano

*Monkey bread is usually served as a sweet dessert (see the Brown Sugar–Pecan Monkey Bread on page 180), but the concept is just as appealing in a savory application. Sweet, buttery biscuit dough is rolled in melted butter and other goodies, then stacked willy-nilly in a skillet and baked to ooey, gooey perfection. Here the biscuits are filled with an herb and cheese mixture and then layered with more cheese for a treat that's as fun to eat as it is delicious.*

1 In a large bowl, combine 2 tablespoons of melted butter, the milk, and the water. Sprinkle the sugar and yeast over the top and stir to mix. Let stand for about 10 minutes, until the mixture becomes frothy.

2 Stir in the flour and salt, using a wooden spoon or your hands, until the dough forms a rough ball. Gently knead the dough until it becomes smooth, about 5 minutes. If the dough is too sticky, add additional flour 1 tablespoon at a time. Place the dough in the bowl, drizzle with the olive oil, cover, and set in a warm spot on your countertop to rise until it is doubled in size, about 90 minutes.

3 Preheat the oven to 350°F.

4 In a small bowl, combine 2 cups of Asiago, ¼ cup of Parmesan, and the garlic, basil, and oregano, and toss to mix. In a separate small bowl, mix together the remaining ½ cup of Asiago and ¼ cup of Parmesan.

**5** Lightly flour a large work surface and then roll the dough out on it into a large rectangle about ⅛-inch thick. Spread the cheese-herb mixture over one half of the dough. Fold the other half over the cheese mixture, pressing it down and sealing it along the open edges.

**6** Using a sharp knife or a pastry or pizza cutter, cut the filled dough into 1-inch squares. Roll each square into a ball.

**7** Brush the sides and bottom of a 10-inch cast iron skillet with melted butter, and pour the remaining ½ cup of butter into a small bowl. Drop a few balls at a time into the melted butter, flipping them over to make sure they are well coated.

**8** Start piling the balls into the skillet, covering the bottom of the skillet in a single layer. Sprinkle some of the reserved Asiago and Parmesan cheese mixture over the layer. Continue dunking and stacking the balls, pressing the new balls into the balls already in the pan. You want the end result to be somewhat haphazard, rather than even layers. When you have a second layer of balls, sprinkle more of the reserved cheese over the top. Continue until all of the balls and cheese are in the skillet.

**9** Transfer the skillet to the oven and bake until golden, about 40 minutes.

**10** Remove the pan from the oven and let cool for a few minutes, then run a knife around the sides of the bread to release it. Invert the bread onto a serving platter, and serve warm.

## CHAPTER 6
# DESSERTS

# RHUBARB SKILLET PIE

SERVES 6 TO 8 ▪ PREP TIME: 15 MINUTES, PLUS 1 HOUR TO CHILL AND COOL
COOK TIME: 30 MINUTES

## FOR THE CRUST

1¼ cups all-purpose flour

1 teaspoon sugar

½ teaspoon kosher salt

½ cup (1 stick) cold, unsalted
butter, cut into pieces

2 to 3 tablespoons ice water

## FOR THE FILLING

5 cups rhubarb, fresh or
frozen (thawed), diced

1¾ cups sugar

6 tablespoons all-purpose flour

Pinch of salt

*Tart rhubarb is almost always combined with a sweeter fruit like strawberries in dessert recipes, but it shines all on its own in this skillet pie. Its tartness cuts through the richness of the pastry crust, making it a refreshing dessert for a spring meal. Serve it with sweetened whipped cream or vanilla ice cream to balance out the tartness of the fruit if you like.*

**To make the crust**

1 In a medium bowl, whisk to combine the flour, sugar, and salt. Add the butter to the flour mixture. Using your hands or a pastry cutter, work the butter into the flour mixture until pea-size clumps form.

2 Stir in the ice water until the dough forms a ball. (You can also make the crust in a food processor. Place the flour, sugar, salt, and butter in the processor, and pulse until pea-size clumps form. With the processor running, add the water in a slow stream until the dough comes together in a ball.)

3 Transfer the dough to a sheet of plastic wrap and press the ball into a rough disk shape. Wrap the dough tightly in the plastic wrap and refrigerate for at least 30 minutes.

**To make the filling and assemble**

1 Preheat the oven to 425°F.

2 In a large bowl, toss together the rhubarb, sugar, flour, and salt. Let stand for 5 minutes.

3 Roll the dough out into a 12-inch circle. Transfer the dough to a 10-inch cast iron skillet. The dough should come partway up the side of the pan. Spoon the rhubarb mixture into the crust and spread it out into an even layer. Fold the edges of the crust over the outside edge of the fruit.

4 Transfer the skillet to the preheated oven and bake for 30 minutes, until the crust is golden and crisp. Remove from the oven and let cool in the pan for at least 30 minutes.

5 Cut into wedges and serve.

SEASONAL SWAP: *If you've got an abundant crop of strawberries to go along with your rhubarb, feel free to substitute 2½ cups diced strawberries for half of the rhubarb.*

# GINGER-PEAR TARTE TATIN

SERVES 8 ▪ PREP TIME: 30 MINUTES IN THE REFRIGERATOR, THEN 10 TO SIT
COOK TIME: 1 HOUR, 10 MINUTES

1¼ cups all-purpose flour

⅔ cup plus 2 tablespoons and
   1 teaspoon sugar, divided

½ teaspoon fine sea salt

¾ cup (1½ sticks) cold,
   unsalted butter, cut into
   pieces, divided

2 to 3 tablespoons ice water

Juice of 1 lemon

5 Bosc pears, peeled, cored,
   and cut into 4 wedges each

1 tablespoon grated
   fresh ginger

*Tarte tatin seems a dessert made for a cast iron skillet. It's like an upside-down tart that starts with caramel made in the hot pan on the stove top. Next a layer of fruit (usually apples or pears) is laid on top. A classic pastry crust is laid over the fruit, and the tart is finished in the oven and then inverted for serving.*

1 Preheat the oven to 375°F.

2 In a medium bowl, whisk to combine the flour, 1 teaspoon of sugar, and the salt. Add ½ cup (1 stick) of the butter to the flour mixture. Using your fingers or a pastry cutter, work the butter into the flour mixture until the mixture resembles peas. Stir in the ice water until the dough forms a ball. (You can also make the crust in a food processor. Place the flour, sugar, salt, and butter in the processor, and pulse until the mixture resembles peas. With the processor running, add the water in a slow stream until the dough comes together in a ball.) Transfer the dough to a sheet of plastic wrap, and press the ball into a rough disk shape. Wrap the dough tightly in the plastic wrap and refrigerate for at least 30 minutes.

3 In a large bowl, squeeze the lemon juice over the pear wedges. Sprinkle 2 tablespoons of sugar and the ginger over the pears, and toss to distribute it evenly.

4 In a 10-inch cast iron skillet over medium heat, melt the remaining ¼ cup (½ stick) of butter. When the butter is completely melted, sprinkle the remaining ⅔ cup of sugar over it, evenly coating the bottom of the pan. Turn off the heat.

5 Arrange the pear wedges in the pan in a decorative, even layer. Heat the pan over medium heat and cook, without stirring, until the caramel turns a deep, golden brown, about 25 minutes. Remove the pan from the heat.

6 Meanwhile, remove the dough from the refrigerator and let sit on the countertop for about 10 minutes. Roll the dough out into a 12-inch circle. Carefully drape the circle of dough over the fruit in the pan (be careful, it's hot!) and, using a spoon or spatula, tuck the edges inside the pan around the fruit.

7 Transfer the skillet to the oven and bake until the crust is golden brown, 35 to 40 minutes.

8 Invert a ceramic or Pyrex pie dish over the skillet and then carefully (very carefully and wearing good oven mitts) turn the skillet and pie dish over so that the tart releases into the pie dish.

9 Let cool to room temperature. Cut into wedges and serve.

PERFECT PAIRING:
*This is a stunning and festive dessert as is, but feel free to top each serving with a dollop of whipped cream, crème fraîche, or vanilla ice cream if you like.*

# PEACH AND BLACKBERRY UPSIDE-DOWN CAKE

SERVES 6 TO 8 ▪ PREP TIME: 15 MINUTES ▪ COOK TIME: 40 MINUTES

3 tablespoons unsalted butter

¼ cup brown sugar

2 cups all-purpose flour

1 teaspoon baking powder

¾ teaspoon fine sea salt

¾ cup (1½ sticks) unsalted butter, at room temperature

¾ cup granulated sugar

2 large eggs

2 teaspoons vanilla extract

3 peaches, pitted and cut into ½-inch wedges

1 cup fresh blackberries

*Peaches and blackberries both hit their peak at the height of summer, and their flavors pair perfectly together to top this simple upside-down cake. Their colors are beautiful together, too. I can imagine few things better than this cake topped with a scoop of vanilla ice cream, enjoyed outside with good friends on a warm summer evening.*

1 Preheat the oven to 350°F.

2 In a 9- or 10-inch cast iron skillet over low heat, melt the butter. Add the brown sugar, stir to combine, and cook until the brown sugar melts. Turn off the heat.

3 In a medium bowl, whisk together the flour, baking powder, and salt. In a large bowl, using an electric mixer, cream the butter and granulated sugar together until fluffy. Add the eggs one at a time, beating after each addition until incorporated. Add the vanilla and beat to incorporate. Add the flour mixture and continue to beat at low speed until the flour is fully incorporated, about 1 minute.

4 Arrange the peaches and blackberries in the melted butter and sugar in the skillet. Cover the entire bottom of the skillet, arranging the peach slices in concentric circles (circles within circles) with the blackberries in between.

5 Drop the batter on top of the fruit by the heaping spoonful. Using the back of the spoon or a spatula, smooth the batter out into an even layer.

6 Transfer the skillet to the oven and bake until the cake is golden on top and a tester inserted into the center comes out clean, 30 to 40 minutes.

7 Remove the cake from the oven and cool until it stops bubbling, just 1 to 2 minutes. Run a knife around the sides of the cake to release it from the skillet. Invert a large platter or cake plate over the skillet and then, very carefully (using oven mitts on both hands) invert the cake onto the plate.

8 Let cool. Serve warm or at room temperature.

**SEASONAL SWAP:** *You can make this cake with virtually any fruit. Apples, pears, persimmons, or figs would all be delightful in the fall. Other spring and summer fruits like strawberries, cherries, plums, or nectarines also work well. And of course, there's always the classic pineapple version.*

# MIXED BERRY CRISP

SERVES 4 ▪ PREP TIME: 10 MINUTES ▪ COOK TIME: 45 MINUTES

1½ cups fresh blackberries

1½ cups fresh raspberries

½ cup fresh blueberries

¼ cup sugar

1 tablespoon cornstarch

1 tablespoon orange juice

1 cup old-fashioned oats

¼ cup all-purpose flour

¼ cup raw almonds,
 finely chopped

¼ cup dark brown sugar

¼ teaspoon fine sea salt

5 tablespoons cold butter,
 cut into small pieces

Vanilla ice cream,
 for serving (optional)

**SEASONAL SWAP:**

*A skillet crisp can be made with just about any fruit. Try it in the fall with pears, apples, and/or persimmons. Use apple juice in place of orange, and add a dash of cinnamon or pumpkin pie spice to the topping mixture.*

*This is the quintessential summer dessert. Full of juicy, sweet berries, topped with a crunchy crisp topping, and, ideally, served with a scoop of rich vanilla ice cream, it is the perfect use for the piles of fresh berries covering stalls in the farmers' market this time of year. Feel free to vary the combination of berries, adding strawberries, boysenberries, gooseberries, or huckleberries, if you like.*

1 Preheat the oven to 350°F.

2 In a large bowl, combine the blackberries, raspberries, and blueberries. Add the sugar, cornstarch, and orange juice, and toss to mix, coating the berries with the sugar and cornstarch.

3 In a medium bowl, stir together the oats, flour, almonds, brown sugar, and salt. Using a fork, a pastry cutter, or your fingers, work the butter into the flour mixture until the mixture resembles peas.

4 Transfer the berry mixture to an 8- or 9-inch cast iron skillet, spreading it out into an even layer. Sprinkle the oat mixture evenly over the top.

5 Transfer the skillet to the oven and bake until the top is crisp and golden and the fruit mixture is bubbling, about 45 minutes.

6 Remove from the oven and let cool for a few minutes before serving. Serve warm, topped with vanilla ice cream (if using).

# STRAWBERRY SHORTCAKE

SERVES 6 ▪ PREP TIME: 20 MINUTES ▪ COOK TIME: 20 MINUTES

2 pounds fresh strawberries, sliced

9 tablespoons sugar, divided

1 tablespoon freshly squeezed lemon juice

2 cups flour

2 teaspoons baking powder

½ teaspoon fine sea salt

¼ teaspoon baking soda

3 cups heavy cream, divided

2 teaspoons vanilla extract

Zest of 1 lemon

*Tender, flaky biscuits topped with ripe fresh strawberries and clouds of sweetened whipped cream, the strawberry shortcake is an iconic American dessert. This stunning dessert is practically synonymous with the imminent arrival of summer, and cooking it in a skillet seems somehow superbly fitting.*

1 In a large bowl, toss together the strawberries, 3 tablespoons of sugar, and the lemon juice. Cover and refrigerate until ready to use.

2 Preheat the oven to 400°F.

3 Into a large bowl or the bowl of a stand mixer, sift the flour, 2 tablespoons of sugar, and the baking powder, salt, and baking soda. Add 1½ cups of cream, and beat at medium-low speed with the electric or stand mixer to combine.

4 Transfer the batter to a 10- or 12-inch cast iron skillet, and smooth it into an even layer that extends all the way to the sides of the pan. Sprinkle 1 tablespoon of sugar over the top. Transfer the skillet to the oven and bake until the top is golden brown, about 20 minutes. Remove the skillet from the oven and cool.

5 In a large bowl using an electric mixer or in the bowl of a stand mixer, beat the remaining 1½ cups cream on medium-high speed until soft peaks form. Add the remaining 3 tablespoons of sugar and the vanilla and lemon zest, and continue to beat at medium-high speed until thick, about 2 minutes.

6 Cut the cake into wedges and spoon some of the strawberries and the accumulated juices over each wedge. Top with dollops of whipped cream and serve.

# SUGAR CREAM PIE

SERVES 8 ▪ PREP TIME: 15 MINUTES, PLUS AT LEAST 1 HOUR TO CHILL
COOK TIME: 1 HOUR, 10 MINUTES

## FOR THE CRUST

1½ cups all-purpose flour,
    plus more for dusting

1 teaspoon granulated sugar

¼ teaspoon fine sea salt

½ cup (1 stick) cold unsalted
    butter, cut into small pieces

4 to 5 tablespoons ice water

## FOR THE FILLING

½ cup granulated sugar

½ cup packed dark
    brown sugar

2 tablespoons all-purpose flour

2 cups heavy cream

½ teaspoon vanilla extract

Powdered sugar, for dusting

*This scrumptious dessert is exactly what it sounds like: a pie filled with a sweet cream custard. It is delightfully simple and absolutely irresistible. The simplicity of the filling really highlights the beauty of a buttery, flaky, skillet-baked pie crust. You could substitute a store-bought crust if you're in a time crunch, but this homemade version is easy to make and tastes divine.*

## To make the crust

1 In a large bowl, whisk together the flour, sugar, and salt. Using a pastry cutter, a fork, or your hands, mix the butter into the flour mixture until it resembles peas. Add 4 tablespoons of ice water, mixing just until the dough comes together. If the mixture is still too dry, add the remaining 1 tablespoon of ice water. Form the dough into a ball and then flatten it into a disk. Wrap tightly in plastic wrap and refrigerate for 30 minutes.

2 Preheat the oven to 400°F.

3 Lightly flour your work surface and roll the dough out into a circle about 12 inches in diameter. Lay the circle in an 8- or 9-inch cast iron skillet. Leave about 1 inch of dough overhanging the edge of the skillet, trimming off and saving the extra. Tuck the overhanging edges inside the rim of the skillet, and crimp the edge all the way around.

4  Line the crust with aluminum foil and fill with dried beans or pie weights. Bake in the preheated oven for 15 minutes. Remove the foil and the beans or weights, and return it to the oven. Cook until the crust is golden brown all over, about 12 minutes more. If there are any cracks in the dough, cover them with the reserved trimmings before you add the filling. Leave the oven at 400°F.

**To make the filling and assemble**

1  In a medium bowl, whisk together the granulated sugar, dark brown sugar, and flour. Break up any clumps with your fingers. In another medium bowl, stir together the cream and vanilla. Add the cream mixture to the sugar mixture in a steady stream, whisking constantly, until well combined and smooth.

2  Pour the filling into the par-baked crust, and return the skillet to the oven. Bake until the filling is set around the edges but still a bit jiggly in the center, about 40 minutes. If the pie looks like it is getting too dark, tent it loosely with foil for the last 10 minutes or so of the baking time.

3  Remove the skillet from the oven and place it on a wire rack to cool. Let cool to room temperature and then refrigerate for at least 30 minutes to fully set the filling.

4  Dust with powdered sugar, slice into wedges, and serve.

**DID YOU KNOW?**
*Sugar cream pie is an American version of a dessert classic from Northern France and Belgium. It was popularized by Quaker settlers in Indiana, where it is commonly known as Hoosier pie, Indiana cream pie, or Indiana farm pie. It can be made with all white sugar or with half or all brown sugar. Maple pie is a sugar cream pie made with maple syrup in place of some of the sugar.*

# BROWN SUGAR–PECAN MONKEY BREAD

SERVES 6 ▪ PREP TIME: 25 MINUTES, PLUS AT LEAST 1 HOUR AND 45 MINUTES TO RISE
COOK TIME: 25 MINUTES

### FOR THE DOUGH

1 cup milk, warmed to 115°F

⅓ cup water, warmed to 115°F

¼ cup granulated sugar

2 tablespoons unsalted butter, melted, plus more for greasing

1 packet (2¼ teaspoons) rapid rise yeast

3¼ cups all-purpose flour, plus more for dusting

2 teaspoons fine sea salt

### FOR THE BROWN SUGAR COATING

½ cup (1 stick) unsalted butter, melted

1 cup packed brown sugar

2½ teaspoons ground cinnamon

½ cup chopped, toasted pecans

*This addictive dessert is easy to make, and tons of fun to eat, pulling apart sweet biscuit chunks drenched with a delightfully buttery, sticky, sweet, cinnamon-y, nutty coating. Rolling and coating all of the balls takes a while, but kids love to help with this part—and they'll definitely appreciate the end result.*

Preheat the oven to 175°F. Once it gets to temperature, turn it off.

**To make the dough**

1 In a small bowl, stir together the milk, water, sugar, butter, and yeast. In a large bowl, mix the flour and salt. Slowly add the milk mixture to the flour mixture, stirring with a wooden spoon, until the dough comes together in a ball. Transfer the ball to a lightly floured work surface and knead it with your hands until it becomes smooth, about 10 minutes.

2 Place the dough ball in a bowl oiled with a bit of melted butter, turning it to coat all over with butter. Cover the bowl and set it in the warm oven (with the heat turned off) to rise until it has doubled in size, about 1 hour.

3 Once the dough has risen, place it on a lightly floured work surface and use a rolling pin to roll it out into an 8-inch square. Mark off roughly 1-inch sections in each direction, so that you end up with 64 small squares (don't worry if they are not perfectly equal in size). Cut along the lines you've marked, and separate the squares. Roll each square into a ball.

**To make the brown sugar coating and assemble**

1 Place the melted butter in a small bowl. In a separate bowl, mix the brown sugar, cinnamon, and pecans.

2 Dip a dough ball into the melted butter, rolling it to make sure it is completely coated, then drop it into the brown sugar mixture, rolling it again to make sure it is completely coated. Place it in a 10- or 12-inch skillet. Repeat with the remaining balls, stacking them tightly in the skillet as you go. Once you have used up all of the dough balls, cover the skillet and place it in the warm oven again for a second rise of about 45 minutes. The dough balls should expand to completely fill the skillet.

3 Remove the skillet from the oven and preheat the oven to 350°F.

4 Bake the monkey bread until browned and cooked through, 22 to 25 minutes.

5 Remove the skillet from the oven and very carefully (with oven mitts on both hands) invert the monkey bread onto a serving platter. Serve warm or at room temperature.

**ESSENTIAL TECHNIQUE:** *If you have a stand mixer, you can save yourself a bit of effort by mixing and kneading the dough in it. Use the dough hook, and oil it before you begin kneading so that the dough doesn't stick to and climb the hook as you mix.*

# CARAMELIZED BANANA–BROWN BUTTER CAKE

SERVES 6 TO 8 ▪ PREP TIME: 15 MINUTES
COOK TIME: 40 MINUTES ▪ TOTAL TIME: 1 HOUR, 5 MINUTES

### FOR THE TOPPING

6 tablespoons butter

¾ cup brown sugar

2 bananas, sliced

### FOR THE CAKE

1 mashed banana

4 tablespoons unsalted butter

1 egg, at room temperature

⅓ cup plain, whole-milk yogurt

½ cup sugar

1 teaspoon vanilla extract

2 teaspoons baking powder

1 teaspoon fine sea salt

1 cup all-purpose flour

*Rich caramel, sweet bananas, and toasty brown butter: Need I say more? This simple cake takes three of the best dessert flavors and turns them into an irresistible topping for a simple banana cake. The heat of the skillet helps caramelize the sugar and bananas to perfection.*

Preheat the oven to 350°F.

**To make the topping**

1 In a 9- or 10-inch cast iron skillet over medium-low heat, melt the butter. Continue to cook, stirring and swirling the pan so that the butter fully coats the bottom, until the butter begins to brown, 5 to 6 minutes.

2 Turn off the heat and sprinkle the brown sugar over the browned butter. Arrange the banana slices on top of the butter and sugar in concentric circles (circles within circles).

**To make the cake**

1 In a large bowl, mix the banana, butter, egg, yogurt, sugar, and vanilla. Add the baking powder, salt, and flour, mixing after each addition until just combined.

2 Pour the cake batter over the bananas in the skillet, and spread it into an even layer with the back of a spoon or spatula.

3 Transfer the skillet to the oven and bake until the top becomes golden brown and the butter-sugar mixture underneath bubbles up around the edges of the cake, about 40 minutes.

4 Remove the skillet from the oven and let cool for about 10 minutes. Run a knife around the sides of the cake to release it. Place a serving platter or cake plate upside down on top of the skillet, then very carefully (with oven mitts on both hands) invert the cake onto the plate.

5 Cut into wedges and serve warm.

SEASONAL SWAP: *We're lucky that we can get ripe, flavorful bananas any time of year, while more delicate fruits are only available, or at least are only any good, in their proper season. In the summertime, make this cake with juicy, ripe peaches instead of bananas. You won't be sorry.*

# CHOCOLATE–PEANUT BUTTER BROWNIES

SERVES 8 ▪ PREP TIME: 10 MINUTES
COOK TIME: 20 MINUTES ▪ TOTAL TIME: 40 MINUTES

4 eggs

1 cup sugar

1 tablespoon vanilla extract

8 ounces dark chocolate, roughly chopped

1 tablespoon coconut oil or butter

½ cup all-purpose flour

2 teaspoons baking powder

½ teaspoon fine sea salt

3 tablespoons peanut butter

*The best part of a rich, chocolatey brownie has got to be the crispy edge, right? Cooking them in a skillet ensures that you get a better-than-average ratio of crispy edge to gooey middle. The peanut butter adds a rich, nutty flavor that makes these brownies hard to resist.*

1 Preheat the oven to 350°F.

2 In a large bowl, whisk together the eggs, sugar, and vanilla.

3 In a small microwave-safe bowl, heat the chocolate and coconut oil in the microwave for 30 seconds, stirring after each burst, until the mixture is smooth. Stir the chocolate mixture into the egg mixture.

4 Into a medium bowl, sift the flour, baking powder, and salt together. Add the flour mixture to the chocolate mixture and stir gently to combine.

5 Transfer the batter to a 10-inch cast iron skillet and smooth the top with a spatula.

6 In a small microwave-safe bowl, heat the peanut butter briefly in the microwave (20 to 30 seconds) to soften it. Dollop the peanut butter onto the brownie batter, then use a chopstick or the handle end of a spoon to swirl it into the batter.

7 Transfer the skillet to the oven and bake for 20 minutes.

8 Remove from the oven and let cool for 10 minutes before serving. Serve warm or at room temperature.

**PERFECT PAIRING:**
*You couldn't go wrong by topping these rich, chocolatey brownies with a scoop of vanilla ice cream or a dollop of whipped cream. On the other hand, a plain glass of milk would also be a perfect accompaniment.*

# S'MORES FOR INDOORS

SERVES 6 ▪ PREP TIME: 10 MINUTES
COOK TIME: 30 MINUTES ▪ TOTAL TIME: 50 MINUTES

- ¾ cup (1½ sticks) unsalted butter, at room temperature, plus more for greasing
- 1 cup (packed) light brown sugar
- 1 cup old-fashioned oats
- ¾ cup all-purpose flour
- ¾ cup (from about 6 crushed whole crackers) graham cracker crumbs
- 1 teaspoon baking powder
- 1 teaspoon fine sea salt
- 2¼ cups mini marshmallows, divided
- 1 cup semisweet chocolate chips

*Everyone knows that s'mores are the best part of camping (wait, everyone does know that, right?), but that doesn't mean you can't enjoy them inside, as well. Crush the graham crackers and turn them into a crisp, buttery crust and a crunchy crumble topping, fill with marshmallows and chocolate, and cook in the oven in your trusty cast iron skillet, and you'll feel like you've been transported to the great outdoors—without having to sleep on the ground.*

1  Preheat the oven to 350°F, and coat the bottom and sides of a 10-inch cast iron skillet with butter.

2  In a large bowl, using an electric mixer set at medium speed, cream together the butter and sugar until fluffy, about 4 minutes. Add the oats, flour, graham cracker crumbs, baking powder, and salt, and beat at medium speed until well combined.

3  Transfer two-thirds of the crumb mixture into the prepared skillet and press it into an even layer that covers the entire bottom. Transfer the skillet to the oven and bake for 5 minutes.

4 Remove the skillet from the oven (leaving the oven on) and scatter 1¾ cups of the marshmallows and the chocolate chips over the crust. Sprinkle the remaining crumb mixture evenly over the top. Scatter the remaining ½ cup of marshmallows over the top.

5 Return the skillet to the oven and bake until the top is golden brown, 20 to 25 minutes. If you want the marshmallows on top to be more toasted, put the skillet under the broiler for about 2 minutes.

6 Let cool for 10 minutes. Cut into wedges and serve warm.

**ESSENTIAL TECHNIQUE:**
*You can make the graham cracker crumbs by pulsing the crackers several times in a food processor or by putting them in a sturdy plastic bag (like a resealable storage bag) and crushing into fine crumbs using a rolling pin or a large can or jar.*

# THE DIRTY DOZEN & THE CLEAN FIFTEEN

A nonprofit and environmental watchdog organization called Environmental Working Group (EWG) looks at data supplied by the US Department of Agriculture (USDA) and the Food and Drug Administration (FDA) about pesticide residues. Each year it compiles a list of the best and worst pesticide loads found in commercial crops. You can use these lists to decide which fruits and vegetables to buy organic to minimize your exposure to pesticides and which produce is considered safe enough to buy conventionally. This does not mean they are pesticide-free, though, so wash these fruits and vegetables thoroughly.

These lists change every year, so make sure you look up the most recent one before you fill your shopping cart. You'll find the most recent lists as well as a guide to pesticides in produce at EWG.org/FoodNews.

## 2016 DIRTY DOZEN

| | | |
|---|---|---|
| Apples | Peaches | *In addition to the dirty dozen, the EWG added two produce contaminated with highly toxic organophosphate insecticides:* |
| Celery | Spinach | |
| Cherries | Strawberries | |
| Cherry Tomatoes | Sweet Bell Peppers | |
| Cucumbers | Tomatoes | |
| Grapes | | Kale/Collard Greens |
| Nectarines | | Hot Peppers |

## 2016 CLEAN FIFTEEN

| | | |
|---|---|---|
| Asparagus | Corn | Mangos |
| Avocados | Eggplant | Onions |
| Cabbage | Grapefruit | Papayas |
| Cantaloupe | Honeydew Melon | Pineapple |
| Cauliflower | Kiwi | Sweet Peas (frozen) |

# MEASUREMENT CONVERSIONS

### VOLUME EQUIVALENTS (LIQUID)

| US STANDARD | US STANDARD (OUNCES) | METRIC (APPROXIMATE) |
| --- | --- | --- |
| 2 tablespoons | 1 fl. oz. | 30 mL |
| ¼ cup | 2 fl. oz. | 60 mL |
| ½ cup | 4 fl. oz. | 120 mL |
| 1 cup | 8 fl. oz. | 240 mL |
| 1½ cups | 12 fl. oz. | 355 mL |
| 2 cups or 1 pint | 16 fl. oz. | 475 mL |
| 4 cups or 1 quart | 32 fl. oz. | 1 L |
| 1 gallon | 128 fl. oz. | 4 L |

### OVEN TEMPERATURES

| FAHRENHEIT (F) | CELSIUS (C) (APPROXIMATE) |
| --- | --- |
| 250° | 120° |
| 300° | 150° |
| 325° | 165° |
| 350° | 180° |
| 375° | 190° |
| 400° | 200° |
| 425° | 220° |
| 450° | 230° |

### VOLUME EQUIVALENTS (DRY)

| US STANDARD | METRIC (APPROXIMATE) |
| --- | --- |
| ⅛ teaspoon | 0.5 mL |
| ¼ teaspoon | 1 mL |
| ½ teaspoon | 2 mL |
| ¾ teaspoon | 4 mL |
| 1 teaspoon | 5 mL |
| 1 tablespoon | 15 mL |
| ¼ cup | 59 mL |
| ⅓ cup | 79 mL |
| ½ cup | 118 mL |
| ⅔ cup | 156 mL |
| ¾ cup | 177 mL |
| 1 cup | 235 mL |
| 2 cups or 1 pint | 475 mL |
| 3 cups | 700 mL |
| 4 cups or 1 quart | 1 L |

### WEIGHT EQUIVALENTS

| US STANDARD | METRIC (APPROXIMATE) |
| --- | --- |
| ½ ounce | 15 g |
| 1 ounce | 30 g |
| 2 ounces | 60 g |
| 4 ounces | 115 g |
| 8 ounces | 225 g |
| 12 ounces | 340 g |
| 16 ounces or 1 pound | 455 g |

# RESOURCES

### WEBSITE

**Lodge Cast Iron**

Lodge is the largest manufacturer of cast iron cookware in the United States. Their website has lots of information about how to use, season, and care for cast iron cookware. www.lodgemfg.com

### BOOKS

Brown, Ellen. *The New Cast Iron Skillet Cookbook: 150 Fresh Ideas for America's Favorite Pan.* New York, NY: Sterling Epicure, 2014.

Cook's Country. *Cook It in Cast Iron: Kitchen-Tested Recipes for the One Pan that Does It All.* Boston, MA: Cook's Country, 2016.

Kramis, Sharon and Julie Hearne. *The Cast Iron Skillet Cookbook: Recipes for the Best Pan in Your Kitchen, 2nd Edition.* Seattle, WA: Sasquatch Books, 2013.

The Lodge Company. *Lodge Cast Iron Nation: Great American Cooking from Coast to Coast.* New York, NY: Oxmoor House, 2014.

# REFERENCES

614 Columbus. "Cooking on the Kitchen Frontier." *614 Columbus.*
Accessed April 4, 2016. 614columbus.com/2015/10
/cooking-on-the-frontier/.

Dillner, Luisa. "Are My Non-stick Saucepans a Health Hazard?"
*The Guardian.* January 25, 2015. Accessed April 4, 2016.
www.theguardian.com/lifeandstyle/2015/jan/25
/are-my-non-stick-pans-a-health-hazard-teflon.

Douglas, Allan. "Cast No Aspersions on Cast-Iron Cookware." *GRIT.*
January 7, 2015. Accessed April 4, 2016. www.grit.com/community
/history/cast-no-aspersions-on-cast-iron-cookware.aspx.

Fears, J. Wayne. *The Complete Book of Dutch Oven Cooking.*
New York, NY: Skyhorse Publishing, 2006.

Ragsdale, John G. *Dutch Ovens Chronicled: Their Use in the United
States.* Fayetteville, AR: University of Arkansas Press, 2016.

Science of Cooking. "Science of Cast Iron Cooking." Accessed
April 4, 2016. www.scienceofcooking.com/cast_iron_cooking.htm.

# RECIPE INDEX

# INDEX